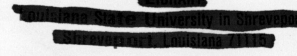

EUGENE   O'NEILL

Modern Literature Monographs

EUGENE O'NEILL

Horst Frenz

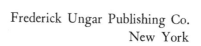Frederick Ungar Publishing Co.
New York

Translated from the German by Helen Sebba
Revisions and additions for the American edition by the author
Published by arrangement with Colloquium Verlag, Berlin

Contents

1

Introduction

While it is legitimate to speak of the two-hundred-year history of the American theater, the first hundred and fifty years of it are of little more than historical interest. Only with the appearance of Eugene O'Neill's plays did American drama reach the level already attained by Poe, Whitman, Melville, and Henry James in other fields of literature. O'Neill's departure from worn-out mediocrity toward a vigorous, creative drama (which soon reached the theaters of the Old World and held its own against the successors of Ibsen and Strindberg) marked the American theater's final break with the old derivative, commercial repertory theater. It marked the end of a hundred and fifty years of lame, high-flown imitations, of star worship, and of the disrespect shown toward theater people. Yet those years cannot be obliterated, and indeed the conditions in which the American theater had to fight for survival remain fundamentally unchanged today. The continuing presence of these conditions will be revealed by a glance at the history of theater in the United States.

In Europe the theater enjoyed a relatively secure position as a kind of stepchild of royal courts and was recognized as a legitimate art form. In America, on the other hand, as recently as two hundred years ago or less, adventurers who took it into their heads to produce plays risked official prosecution. Such "good-for-nothings" were denounced with abhorrence for their "unchristian and profane conduct." In 1709 "boxing matches and performances of plays" were rigorously prohibited in New York. Laws of this kind were soon repealed of course, and even in Puritan New England boxing matches and performances of plays soon ceased to be classed in the same category. Nevertheless it was many years before the trades of acting and playwriting became respectable.

In the second half of the eighteenth century theater life began to acquire a stronger foothold. Until then there had been nothing but traveling companies, many of them English, which performed in makeshift theaters. Now the first permanent theaters were built—in Philadelphia in 1766, in New York in 1767, in Boston in 1794 —and the number of American companies quickly increased. American dramatists began to write for these theaters, though most often their work consisted chiefly in translating and adapting European plays, principally French ones, and they were usually content to follow the techniques and themes of European melodramas. The first American characters to be introduced—the noble Indian, the faithful Negro slave—soon became popular stereotypes that reappeared almost unchanged from one play to the next. The first play that attempted to be specifically American was Royall Tyler's *The Contrast* (1787), in which American virtues victoriously confront European craftiness. Its technique is closely modeled on that of Richard Sheridan.

In the nineteenth century, American drama began to deal more adequately with the life style and problems of Americans, but these attempts were still eclipsed by purely commercial plays and achieved little success before the beginning of the twentieth century.

As technique became more sophisticated, staging became more spectacular. Sensational effects were sometimes introduced into standard melodramas. In Au-

gustine Daly's *Under the Gaslight* (1867), for instance,
the hero was tied to railroad tracks as a full-size locomo-
tive bore down upon him—the "theater of the *dernier
cri*," which, although a passing fashion, commanded
great popularity.

It was a long time before democratic America
brought forth wealthy patrons of the arts, and even then
the theater profited from them only sporadically. Theater had to compete then, as it has to compete today, on
equal terms with other forms of entertainment—in those
days with circuses, revues, and burlesque, today with
movies and television. As a result theater tended to offer
the same kind of attractions, so that the distinction between entertainment and art was blurred. Of course
measures were taken from time to time to preserve the
independence and dignity of the serious theater, but the
tastes of the paying audiences usually won out. A first
wave of realistic drama with higher literary aims, exem-
plified by the plays of James A. Herne, waned. The star,
not the work, was the center of interest, both in the
legitimate theater and in American opera. Names such as
Thomas A. Cooper, Edwin Forrest, Edwin and John
Wilkes Booth, and later the Barrymores were the chief
attraction for the majority of audiences. New York became the theatrical center and the arbiter of taste in
drama as well as opera and light entertainment.

The situation at the end of the nineteenth century offered little hope for the emergence of a successful na-
tional drama of international significance. In Europe at
the turn of the century the Théâtre Libre in Paris, the
Freie Bühne in Berlin, the Abbey Theatre in Dublin,

Strindberg's Intimate Theater, and Stanislavsky's productions in Moscow had reached new heights of serious experimentation and artistic maturity. In the United States, however, the theater was controlled or at least dominated by the technique, artistic concepts, and outdated extravagances of such people as David Belasco, who cared little about literary quality, although their productions were marvels of technical sophistication and realistic detail.

Many people recognized that these conditions were restrictive and detrimental to the development of serious dramatic art, whether operatic or theatrical, and tried to counteract them, but they were—and still are—so firmly rooted in the democratic principle of free competition that broadly speaking only two solutions existed. One was to change or eliminate the commercial basis of the serious theater by means of subventions—something that has never been achieved or even attempted in a radical way. The other was the kind of breakthrough that only a dramatist whose work combined literary quality with wide audience appeal could bring about. Eugene O'Neill was this dramatist, and the breakthrough that he initiated was consolidated later by others of his stature. Nevertheless, fundamental conditions of existence in the American theater remained unchanged. O'Neill and others after him managed by means of fierce pertinacity to work in spite of them, but they did not eliminate them, and it is essential to remember this if we hope to understand either O'Neill himself or the American theater in general.

2

Years of

Apprenticeship

Eugene O'Neill's plays have found a wider audience and are more frequently performed in Europe than in their native America. If we look to European criticism for an explanation of this remarkable fact, we are continually reminded that audiences there found traces of their own tradition in his work and recognized the relationship between dramatic movements familiar to them and O'Neill's plays. Nevertheless, in evaluating O'Neill it would be wrong to attach too much importance to his European reputation. Essentially he belongs to the tradition of the American theater, to which he brought new stimulus and against which he waged a successful revolution. While European dramatists and trends have left their mark on him, what he derived from them is far outweighed by factors such as his own contrariness, his liking for experiment, and his exceptional experience of life.

Eugene Gladstone O'Neill was born—one might almost say born into the American theater—on 16 October 1888, in New York City. His father was James O'Neill, an actor who in the 1880s had won fame and fortune in the role of the Count of Monte Cristo. This son of Irish immigrants had risen from modest circumstances to success, both material and professional, as an actor, but his fear of poverty enslaved him to this one successful yet artistically inferior role. He played it for more than twenty years, at first because he enjoyed the applause and the money, but later reluctantly and with growing bitterness over his inability to break away from it. For the American audience he *was* the Count of Monte Cristo. This was the role they wanted to see him in, and all his efforts to act in better roles were unavailing.

The way of life of the O'Neill family was that of the family of a road-company star, constantly on the move. Ella O'Neill, a sheltered girl who had had a convent education, had fallen in love with, and married, the hero-star. The disillusionment was too much for her. An alimony suit brought against her husband soon after their marriage and the malicious publicity accompanying it, the instability of life in a road company, her husband's drinking, and finally the death of her second child were possible factors that led her to become addicted to morphine.

O'Neill's late autobiographical play, *Long Day's Journey into Night*, presents a harrowing portrait of this family as seen by a retrospective mind in search of self-justification: a family tormented by its past and its missed opportunities, a family in which each member blames the other while each clings to his own distorted illusions. In the play James Tyrone (James O'Neill) and his wife attribute their fate to the curse of the theater, which directly or indirectly prevented the father from achieving artistic success, interfered with the happiness of the family, and was partly responsible for the death of the child.

Eugene O'Neill sought to free himself from the constraint of this past, but it was only toward the end of his life that he resorted to direct autobiographical statement. In earlier works such as *The Straw* and *Ah, Wilderness!* the autobiographical element is veiled rather than explicit. But from the very start he openly attacked the commercial American theater and its successful mediocrity. Revolt against the circumstances of his personal life also meant revolt against the world of James

O'Neill—the American theater of the late nineteenth century. Nonetheless, it was only late in life that he embarked upon a direct creative confrontation of the past.

Around the turn of the century Eugene's older brother James, or Jamie as he was called, joined their father's company after a promising apprenticeship. Both sons had traveled with their parents for many years, with interludes at boarding schools. Eugene used to say that he grew up in the wings and couldn't see life with a touring company as being such a marvelous thing. "My early experience with the theater," he said later, "really made me revolt against it. As a boy I saw so much of the old, ranting, artificial romantic stuff that I always had a sort of contempt for the theater." Eugene was not attracted to the theater; in fact he did not seem to be particularly attracted to anything. He attended Princeton from 1906 to 1907, but left because he was about to be suspended on account of "an escapade." Jamie introduced him to night life—so far as he needed any introduction. In those years Eugene's life was devoted to drinking, girls, and anarchists; his favorite reading was Nietzsche's *Thus Spake Zarathustra*. He had no regular occupation, and after he had been working for a few weeks for a mail-order house, his father, determined to prevent his son's marriage to a certain Kathleen Jenkins, arranged for him to accompany a married couple on a gold-prospecting expedition to Honduras. In October 1909, Eugene sailed from San Francisco on a banana boat, having secretly married Kathleen Jenkins just before he left.

All Eugene got out of the trip was malaria. He was back in New York after six and a half months. A newspaper announcement of the birth of his son Eugene Gladstone O'Neill reminded him that he was married, but he felt no obligation to fulfill his duties as husband and father and went off on tour with his father's company. This new association with the theater was no more productive than the earlier ones were. He left the company as soon as he could and signed on as a crew member of the Norwegian sailing vessel *Charles Racine* in Boston.

Eugene left the ship in Buenos Aires, but this first voyage introduced him to a world whose atmosphere was to pervade his early work, the so-called sea plays. His stay in Buenos Aires (interrupted by a voyage to South Africa) deepened his knowledge of the world of derelicts, loafers, and exiles. Eugene slept on park benches or on the beach and associated with other down-and-outs. He tried various kinds of work but stuck to none and finally returned to New York on the British steamer *Kalis*, which was to be the model for the S.S. *Glencairn* of the sea plays.

Eugene did not get in touch with his family but lived in a saloon and rooming house on the New York waterfront known as Jimmy the Priest's. This refuge for unemployed seamen, prostitutes, and other outcasts of society appears in *Anna Christie* as Johnny the Priest's and later became the setting for *The Iceman Cometh*. Many of O'Neill's fellow lodgers also appear in his plays. *The Iceman Cometh* contains a whole collection of them. At one point he broke off his drinking and loafing to ship on a passenger liner bound for England and spent some time in English waterfront dives before returning to

Jimmy the Priest's. In the meantime his wife sued for divorce, and O'Neill provided the court with the only ground accepted by the state of New York in those days: notarized evidence from a brothel at 148 West Forty-fifth Street.

In 1912 Eugene became a reporter on the New London (Connecticut) *Telegraph*, but he was not very productive journalistically. The poems he published at regular intervals showed no particular talent. His first drafts of one-act plays apparently date from this period, although O'Neill himself denied this. Certainly he did not seriously entertain the idea of becoming a playwright until the end of 1912, when tuberculosis forced him to enter the Gaylord Farm sanatorium. O'Neill always insisted that the months he spent in this institution were a turning point in his life. Cut off from the escape of alcohol and the company of the kind of people who lived at Jimmy the Priest's and forced into a new life style of rest and regular hours—which was no doubt intolerable to him at first—he began to read and write.

The casually acquired chaotic experiences of his life up to this point had a chance to sort themselves out, to establish relationships, and to mature into future themes. They could be chiseled into shape and looked at objectively; they began to demand analysis. But this new intellectual activity required time for concentration. After a short story entitled "Tomorrow," he wrote several drafts for one-act plays but finished only one, *A Wife for a Life*, the action of which takes place against the background of O'Neill's jungle experiences in Honduras. This somewhat flat first attempt shows a characteristic that appears again and again throughout O'Neill's work: the autobiographical element. In *A Wife for a Life* this tendency is well to the fore—almost to the point of ego-centricity. A young gold prospector falls in love with the wife of his older partner, who turns her over to him as though upholding the motto "greater love hath no man than that he giveth his wife for his friend!" The play is rather sentimental, rather unbelievable, and the monologues are a little too long, but it is concise and well-resolved, simple and unpretentious.

O'Neill was released from the sanatorium after six months. He returned to New London, where he finished several more one-acters, including *Abortion, The Movie Man*, and *The Sniper*, as well as the three-act *Servitude*. All his attempts to interest producers and publishers in the one-acters were to no avail, and his father finally offered to pay for the printing of a small 168-page volume entitled *Thirst, and Other One-Act Plays*. Few copies were sold, and only one journal reviewed it. Clayton Hamilton, a friend of O'Neill's, wrote in *The Bookman* of April 1915: "[O'Neill reveals] a keen sense of the reactions of character under stress of violent emotion; and his dialogue is almost brutal in its power."

O'Neill destroyed several of his plays. He was so uncertain of his ability as a dramatist that in 1914 he registered to be admitted to the famous drama workshop, English 47, given by Professor George Pierce Baker, Harvard's famous specialist in drama, and went off to Cambridge with the intention of becoming "an artist or nothing." He was one of the few applicants to be accepted for the following year's advanced course but changed his mind shortly before the beginning of the semester, perhaps because Professor Baker did not show any enthusiasm for the one-acter *Bound East for Cardiff*, which he submitted along with his application.

O'Neill now lived mostly in or near Greenwich Village, and for months at a time did little but drink in the company of artists, drifters, anarchists, and prostitutes. The Greenwich Village of those days had something of the aura of the Left Bank of Paris—at least for the young intellectuals and artists who in 1914 founded the Washington Square Players for the purpose of voicing a protest against the commercial Broadway theater and launching young American dramatists in one-act plays.

Most of the group's members were short on theatrical experience but long on idealism. Among them were George Cram (Jig) Cook and his wife Susan Glaspell, but they soon withdrew because the group was not revolutionary enough for them. Having had their play, a "Freudian comedy" entitled *Suppressed Desires*, rejected by the Washington Square group, Cook and his wife founded their own group in Cape Cod in 1916. This new group, called the Provincetown Players, opened with a performance of *Suppressed Desires* in a fish house (the "Wharf Theater") on a Provincetown wharf. Shortly thereafter, the Provincetown Players moved to Greenwich Village, and during the second half of the decade they coexisted with the Washington Square Players in New York.

Although the life span of these two groups was relatively short (the Washington Square Players disbanded in 1918; the Provincetown Players ceased production in 1921, reopened in 1924, then failed and disbanded after moving to the Garrick Theater in 1929), both were instrumental in initiating O'Neill's career. The emergence of these two "little theater" groups, especially their performances of O'Neill's early works, marks a major turning point in the development of the modern American theater.

Although at this time O'Neill was moving restlessly between Provincetown and Greenwich Village, he was not yet in touch with either of these amateur groups. However, the Provincetowners, whose own writers could not provide all the plays they needed, were looking for works by younger American dramatists, and he inevitably came to their attention. Terry Carlin, a philosopher-drifter who was one of O'Neill's drinking companions, was asked by Susan Glaspell if he couldn't write a play for the Provincetown Players. His answer was: "No, I don't write. I just think and sometimes talk. But O'Neill has a whole trunkful of plays."

A reading was arranged, and the group heard the one-acter *Bound East for Cardiff*, which Professor Baker had not thought highly of when O'Neill had submitted it for the famous drama workshop. But the Provincetown Players immediately accepted it, and produced it a few weeks later. *Bound East for Cardiff* became their first success. The play, which takes place on board ship and deals with the last moments in the life of the seaman Yank, is almost without plot and gains its effects entirely from atmosphere, simple, true-to-life characters, and a kind of naturalistic speech unknown in American drama of the time. During the same season, the summer of 1916, the Provincetowners produced O'Neill's *Thirst*, another sea play, which, however, was not so enthusiastically received. O'Neill played minor roles in both plays: the second mate in *Bound East for Cardiff* and a sailor in *Thirst*.

With the beginning of his association with the Provincetown Players in 1916, O'Neill had taken the step that separates theoretical and practical dramatists. He helped with the production and was able to try out his ideas in practice. Moreover, in the Provincetowners he had found a group of competent and enthusiastic supporters who were ready, after this success, to implement his plans with dedication.

3

Breakthrough

When the Provincetown Players moved to Greenwich Village in 1916, they revived O'Neill's *Bound East
for Cardiff* and produced his *Before Breakfast*, a one-
acter with a love-hate theme reminiscent of Strindberg's
The Stronger, written in a similar monologue technique.
But O'Neill's work still made no impact on the New
York press. Productions of *The Sniper* and *Fog* followed, but *Bound East for Cardiff* was his only notable
achievement during the company's first New York season.

Back in Provincetown, O'Neill wrote four one-act
plays in quick succession, all of which are still occasionally performed: *The Moon of the Caribbees*, *Ile*, *The
Long Voyage Home*, and *In the Zone*. Like many of his
short plays, these are as rich in atmosphere as they are
limited in action. In the sea plays especially he created
a mood of fascinating authenticity. The tension of *In the
Zone* held the audience spellbound. The incessant offstage sound effects in *The Moon of the Caribbees* anti-
cipated the drums of *The Emperor Jones*. Even in these
early plays the characters' ordinariness, their resigned
lostness, made them much more effective than the
standard characters of traditional drama.

In 1917, O'Neill began a friendship with George
Jean Nathan, publisher with H. L. Mencken of *The
Smart Set*. This magazine specialized in literary controversy and profiles debunking outstanding theatrical
figures such as Augustus Thomas, a successful and pro-
lific writer of plays of wide popular appeal. Nathan was
undogmatic, versatile, and unprejudiced, and he played,
partly through his support of O'Neill, an important part

in the American theater's change of direction. It was he who exploded the myth of Augustus Thomas being a great dramatist and he never stopped trying to shake the smug Broadway colossus out of its materialist lethargy. When O'Neill showed him the manuscripts of *The Long Voyage Home, Ile,* and *The Moon of the Caribbees,* Nathan recognized a talent worth encouraging, and he was soon convinced that he had discovered the first really significant American dramatist. In a move which went beyond O'Neill's most optimistic hopes, *The Smart Set* published all three plays between October 1917 and August 1918.

In October 1917 the Washington Square Players produced *In the Zone,* which the Provincetowners had turned down as "not experimental enough." This production brought O'Neill to the attention of the New York critics. The action, like that of most of his plays of this period (some of which were later combined in a cycle entitled *S.S. Glencairn*) takes place on board ship, in this case a freighter passing through the zone of German submarine activity. The crew's anxiety finds an outlet in hostility toward a seaman whom they suspect of being a German spy because he jealously guards a locked black box. The tension rises to a climax when they break open the box only to find that it contains a bundle of old love letters, relics of a tragic life. The play may have owed some of its success to the German submarine scare, which at that time was constantly in the minds of the inhabitants of the East Coast and in the newspapers. Certainly *In the Zone* was much less successful when it was revived after the war.

Toward the end of 1917 O'Neill met Agnes Boulton, a twenty-four-year-old writer of unpretentious novellas and short stories, which appeared chiefly in pulp magazines. Six months later they were married in Provincetown. In 1919 they moved into an abandoned Coast Guard station nearby, which Eugene's father had bought for them "in anticipation of his first grandchild."

Negotiations were in progress for a Broadway production of *Beyond the Horizon*, but it was two years before the play was staged, and O'Neill's disappointment at the delay was all the more acute because he believed a Broadway triumph to be within his grasp. In the meantime he wrote several one-act plays: *Shell Shock* (later destroyed), *Where the Cross Is Made*, and *The Dreamy Kid*. The last two were produced by the Provincetowners during the 1918–19 season. *Where the Cross Is Made* made its debut at their new theater at 133 McDougal Street. In this play O'Neill failed in his attempt to make the audience share the hallucinations of the characters by means of phantoms on stage. The critics were unimpressed, and the play received very poor notices.

A production of *The Moon of the Caribbees* a short time later did not fare much better, but this did not prevent its being published in book form in June 1919, together with six other sea plays (reissued in 1940 as *The Long Voyage Home: Seven Plays of the Sea*).

O'Neill was still waiting for John D. Williams to produce *Beyond the Horizon*. Williams, one of the few Broadway producers who would occasionally disregard commercial considerations where plays of literary value were concerned, had accepted this three-act play on

George Jean Nathan's enthusiastic recommendation, but it was many months before he decided to produce it. About this time, *Chris Christopherson*, O'Neill's second three-act play, and *The Straw* were accepted by another Broadway producer, George Tyler, a friend of Eugene's father. Unfortunately Tyler had no immediate plans for producing them, and O'Neill, who was ready to take Broadway by storm, found himself in the intolerable situation of having three plays accepted by Broadway producers and yet having to sit back and wait endlessly while he felt his chances of triumph were ebbing away.

In October 1919 the Provincetowners opened their third season with *The Dreamy Kid*, the story of a young Negro gangster on the run from the police who goes to see his dying mother and is arrested at her deathbed. The critics' favorable reaction was partly due to the fact that Ida Rauh, the director, had cast members of a Harlem Negro company in the roles that would normally have been played by white actors in blackface. (Their success led O'Neill to cast Negroes in the black roles in his later plays *The Emperor Jones* and *All God's Chillun Got Wings*.) Otherwise the play received scant recognition, although the famous critic Alexander Woollcott declared, in *The New York Times* of 9 November 1919, that O'Neill "induces your complete sympathy and pity for a conventionally abhorrent character." For all its bright promise, the year 1919 did not after all see O'Neill established on Broadway. It is doubtful that the birth of his second son, Shane, was much consolatión, for O'Neill was an indifferent father all his life.

In the end, plans to produce *Beyond the Horizon*

materialized quite suddenly and unexpectedly. Richard Bennett, who was appearing in Elmer Rice's *For the Defense* (first produced at the Playhouse Theater on 19 December 1919), read the manuscript and was so impressed by it that he suggested to Williams that they perform it at matinees during the run of *For the Defense,* with the possibility of introducing evening performances at some later date. Williams agreed, and Bennett assembled a cast consisting chiefly of actors appearing in *For the Defense.*

Beyond the Horizon (1920), O'Neill's first full-length play, clearly shows the influence of the naturalist theater. Instead of traditional, symbolically simplified stage settings, he uses a profusion of realistic detail (including extremely long stage directions) to depict, for instance, the Mayo family's progressive disillusionment. Robert Mayo, who is about to realize his dream of journeying "beyond the horizon," of going to sea, suddenly throws himself into a new dream of marital happiness with his neighbor's daughter. His brother Andrew, whose love for the girl is rejected, undertakes the sea journey in his place. Thus the two brothers exchange plans: Robert embraces a new dream in his decision to remain at home, while Andrew seeks a new life beyond the horizon.

Both are failures; both are made to suffer the consequences of the betrayal of their respective dreams. Robert, relinquishing his romantic quest for the beauty and poetry of life beyond the horizon, dies in disillusionment on the farm. Andrew, repulsed by the life of a seaman, fails in his South American business venture. Like the brothers, Ruth, Robert's wife, realizes too late that she made the wrong choice. Her marriage is a failure, and the romantic notions that had accompanied it are soon swept away by the stark realities of farm life.

O'Neill presents the two brothers as opposite types who fail to achieve their respective ideals of happiness in each other's dreams. No one is able to realize his dream of the future, no one is able to get what he really wants. Robert finally realizes that sailing "beyond the horizon" can be achieved only through death. For the living, the happiness that lies beyond the horizon remains an unattainable illusion.

The authenticity of the characters, their complexity (which does not make them any less pitiful), their gradual, convincing development, their inhibitions and Chekhovian inability to relate to each other—these were subtleties new to the American theater, at least in this masterful form. They made it easier to overlook the play's technical defects and the somewhat clumsy way in which acts and scenes had been divided. *Beyond the Horizon* can hardly be expected to measure up to *Mourning Becomes Electra* or *The Iceman Cometh*. Nevertheless, when it was first performed the critics had good reason to speak of the opening of a new era in the American theater. The play won the Pulitzer Prize in 1920. O'Neill, the second dramatist to receive the prize (previously awarded to Jesse Lynch Williams), remarked that this was the first he had heard of its existence, let alone the thousand-dollar check that went with it.

Encouraged by the success of *Beyond the Horizon*,

George Tyler decided to produce *Chris Christopherson* on Broadway as soon as possible. However, he was cautious enough to arrange out-of-town tryouts, and it opened in Atlantic City with Emmett Corrigan and Lynn Fontanne in the leading roles. Most of the critics liked it, but the public was less enthusiastic. O'Neill had already revised it extensively, and he now suggested rewriting the love scene between Anderson (the first mate who was to become Matt Burke) and Anna, and getting rid of the conventional, superficial happy ending. But the reception the play received in Philadelphia was not good enough to warrant a Broadway production, and Tyler dropped it and made plans to produce *The Straw* instead.

O'Neill decided to revise *Chris Christopherson* drastically and to make its focal point not Chris but the sea as a force that shapes men's destinies. But Tyler still hesitated to produce the play in New York.

A completely new version entitled *Anna Christie* was finally staged on 10 November 1921—in ideal circumstances. Arthur Hopkins, a leading director, became its sponsor and produced it at the Vanderbilt Theater. Pauline Lord, an established Broadway star, played Anna, and Hopkins's press agent arranged for some useful publicity. *Anna Christie* was a popular success, and the critics received it with admiration and encouragement.

In *Anna Christie* (1921), O'Neill combined symbolic and realistic elements, as he was to do later in *The Iceman Cometh*. In its sympathetic treatment of a prostitute, the main figure Anna, the play reflects the

influence of the naturalist drama of the late nineteenth
century. As a child, Anna had been sent to live in Minnesota, in order to protect her from the ominous influence of the sea. Her father Chris, repeatedly referring
to "dat ole davil sea," cannot or will not escape this
influence.

The play opens with Anna's arrival on the waterfront, where, recovering from an illness, she plans to
visit her father, a sea captain. Concealing her past, Anna
finds, aboard her father's vessel, the sense of freedom
and cleanness she longs for, and falls in love, for the
first time, with the stoker Matt Burke. Ignoring the dis-
approving Chris, the two plan to marry. But when
Burke discovers the truth concerning Anna's past, his
illusion of love and future happiness is shattered, and
he deserts her to take refuge in the illusions induced by
whiskey. Yet, upon Burke's drunken return, Anna's love
and willingness to reform convince him of the possibility of a successful marriage. The somewhat unbelievable
happy ending within this naturalistic milieu is realized
in the reunion of the lovers with Chris's approval and
blessing. The "ole davil sea" has been defeated by the
forces of love and human understanding. Yet, as the
curtain descends, Chris remarks: "Fog, fog, fog, all
bloody time. You can't see vhere you vas going, no.
Only dat ole davil sea—she knows!"

O'Neill presents his characters as blind and power-
less victims in the face of destiny, helplessly adrift in
life, and subject to forces over which they have no control. Only in love and mutual trust can hope be found.

The critics assumed that this happy ending repre-

sented O'Neill's own idea of how such a situation might
"come out all right." They accused him of wriggling out
of the problem by means of a conventional compromise
and found the happy ending irreconcilable with the in-
compatibility of the characters and everything in their
past lives that would inevitably separate them in the
future. Some of them hinted that O'Neill had abandoned
his original principles as a sop to popular taste. (It is
interesting to recall that in the first German production
of *Anna Christie* in Berlin in 1923 O'Neill's happy ending was replaced by a tear-jerking "tragic" one in which
Anna—without the least motivation—suddenly draws a
pistol, shoots herself in the temple, and dies with a whis-
pered "goodbye," as the seamen bend over her, mur-
muring, "Poor girl.")

O'Neill had always detested and implacably fought
the commercialism of Broadway, and nothing was better
calculated to ruin his pleasure in his success than im-
putations of this kind. He was quite justifiably angry
at the critics' failure to see that he was not expressing
his own belief in the compromise reached by Anna,
Matt, and Chris, but was showing that they, by believing
it, were once more committing themselves to an illusion.
His reaction was to call *Anna Christie* the worst failure
he had experienced. Assuming that it owed its popular
success entirely to the happy ending, he issued a statement defending his play and his honor as a dramatist.
But he had lost all enthusiasm for it—in spite of the
second Pulitzer Prize it won him.

The Straw was produced at the same time as *Anna
Christie*. In *The Straw*, which deals with O'Neill's ex-

periences in the sanatorium, Eileen Carmody, uprooted from the bourgeois life in which she had her own place and her own responsibilities, finds herself with nothing to do but wait, fret, grow bored, and worry about her weight. As in Thomas Mann's *Magic Mountain*, this new world begins to efface her old life, which recedes as her connections with it grow tenuous and break. Eileen hopes to find a new life "outside" through a fellow patient, but he does not reciprocate her love and leaves the sanatorium. From this moment on illness and life, weight, temperature, and hope become identical, and Eileen becomes moribund. The man she loves finally returns, recognizes his "duty," and from one minute to the next falls in love with the dying girl. This is a flaw in the play: his change of heart is unconvincing and apparently unmotivated. Nevertheless, in this final scene of tragic, unresolved conflict between hope, will, and medically inevitable death, O'Neill does manage to arouse the audience to pity. Although the reviews were generally favorable, the play was rightly judged inferior to *Beyond the Horizon* and *Anna Christie*. Alexander Woollcott wrote, in *The New York Times* of 11 November 1921, that while *The Straw* was below the level of O'Neill's best plays, "it still has enough of his force and his quality to make it worth seeing." While the first-night audience at the Greenwich Village Theater, "keen and overexpectant," found the play "interesting and moving," the general public did not take to it, partly because of its hopeless atmosphere and the naturalistic portrayal of sanatorium life.

Nevertheless O'Neill had seen his name in the lights

of Broadway, and there was no longer any doubt that
he was one of America's most promising young dramatists. James O'Neill, whose attitude to his son's "scrib-
bling" had been skeptical, saw Eugene launched upon
his great career before he died in 1920, after an illness
of two months. One might say that the O'Neill family
typified within itself the American theater's abrupt
change of direction. The death of James O'Neill marked
the passing of one of the last great representatives of
pompous, spectacular, financially profitable theater, at
the very moment when Eugene O'Neill, who was to give
American drama a new style and raise it to international
stature, was enjoying his first successes.

4

Expressionistic Experiments

In 1920, O'Neill read to the Cooks a play entitled "The Silver Bullet," which later became *The Emperor Jones*. Jig Cook's stage sense and imagination immediately grasped its possibilities. He presented it to the Provincetowners with enthusiasm, and got them to believe that this would be the biggest venture the company had ever undertaken. He coaxed them to invest their total capital of five hundred dollars in sets, and with his own hands he began to build out of iron bars and plaster a version of O'Neill's vision of a primeval forest dome.

A circus performer had told O'Neill the story of President Sam, dictator of Haiti, who spread the rumor that he was immune to ordinary lead bullets and could be killed only by a silver one, and who was finally hacked to pieces. O'Neill combined this figure with another Haitian dictator, a Negro slave named Henri Christophe who proclaimed himself emperor of part of Haiti and finally committed suicide. Onto this basic idea he grafted the image, probably inspired by his own experiences in Honduras, of the primeval forest menacingly closing in on the emperor and cutting off his escape. At one point he came across a book on religious rites in the Congo, and for over a year and a half his mind was preoccupied with the idea of using the drum as a symbol of pursuit:

From the distant hills comes the faint, steady thump of a tom-tom, low and vibrating. It starts at a rate exactly corresponding to normal pulse beat—72 to the minute—and continues at a gradually accelerating rate from this point uninterruptedly to the very end of the play. [Stage direction, *The Emperor Jones*, scene one]

Would the audience too succumb to its spell? Jig Cook was not the only one to be fascinated by the result. The tropical forest was constructed and made to seem impenetrably dense by sophisticated lighting techniques.

Once again the unwritten law of the white theater that Negro roles must be played by white actors in blackface was broken, as it had been in *The Dreamy Kid*. For the role of Brutus Jones, the Provincetowners invited Charles S. Gilpin, a part-time actor with experience in vaudeville and Negro stock companies. Gilpin scored a personal triumph in the role, which he repeated on Broadway and on tour until his performance grew so careless that he was replaced by Paul Robeson.

The Emperor Jones (1920) dramatizes the psychological process by which Brutus Jones, the self-proclaimed emperor of an island in the West Indies, regresses from the civilized state of his present consciousness to the primitive state of his personal unconscious and the collective unconscious of his race. The impetus of this regression is fear, which pervades the entire play. Both the setting and the time of the action of the play's eight scenes correspond to the stages of Jones's psychological regression through the various levels of his mind. From the security of his colorful, illuminated palace—the facade of his civilized superiority and authority, based on the natives' superstition that he can be killed only by a silver bullet—Jones is forced to flee the island when his subjects rebel. The first scene, taking place in the palace during midafternoon, serves as an exposition of the circumstances of Jones's escape from an American chain gang, his flight to the West Indies, and his subsequent rise to power. Jones's attempt to flee the rebellious natives, presented in scenes two through seven, leads him progressively deeper into the forest and deeper into the night. Throughout these six scenes, his mounting fear is intensified by the beat of the natives' tom-tom, which grows increasingly louder and quicker, while his gradual disrobing, which he feels will facilitate his flight through the forest, indicates his regression to a primitive state. In these scenes, Jones is confronted with a series of pantomimic visions induced by his growing fear. These visions are projections from the increasingly deeper levels of his mind, from his immediate, conscious awareness (scene two: the "little formless fears"), through the experiences of his personal past (scenes three and four: the murder he had committed and his imprisonment), to his racial or collective unconscious (scenes five and six: the slave auction and the slave ship), and finally culminating in a primitive rite of human sacrifice (scene seven). In the eighth scene, which, like the first scene, serves an expository function, the play concludes with a return to daylight on the edge of the forest, as Jones's corpse is brought in by the natives.

O'Neill's preoccupation with shattering the external reality perceived by the conscious mind for the sake of expressing the inner reality of the subconscious mind, and the stage effects he employed to achieve this end, indicate a strong affinity between his Expressionist experiments and the plays of the German Expressionists. Although O'Neill denied the possibility of a direct literary influence, one may point to the many parallels and striking similarities between his works and those of Georg Kaiser, the most representative Expressionist playwright. O'Neill had seen the New York production of Kaiser's *From Morn to Midnight*, but only after he had written *The Emperor Jones*. He read Kaiser's play before writing *The Hairy Ape*, his second major Expressionist experiment, but he had already "planned" his play.

Aside from the questions of literary influence, a comparison of *The Emperor Jones* and *From Morn to Midnight*, considering their differences as well as their similarities, brings into focus the nature of O'Neill's "Expressionism." Thematically, both plays deal with the externalization of internal, emotional states, the radical, subjective transformation of objective reality as the result of an extreme psychological crisis. The central figure in each play is driven by an overwhelming emotional force, which, growing increasingly stronger, finally shatters the conscious, rational control of the intellect in the apprehension of reality. The dynamic power of the subconscious obliterates the superficial facade of objective reality, as O'Neill's emperor and Kaiser's bank teller reach the limits of the intensification of psychological experience. Both are hunted men; in the jungle scenes in *The Emperor Jones* and in the snow scene in Kaiser's *From Morn to Midnight* they are wandering through a threatening world, pursued by visions. Structurally, O'Neill's play, like that of Kaiser, adheres to the form of the "station drama," initiated by Strindberg and later adopted by the German Expressionists. Nevertheless, important differences between O'Neill and Kaiser

clearly indicate that the American playwright was not
merely an imitator of European models. O'Neill was primarily concerned with the individual, rather than with
the masses of the industrial society. Unlike Kaiser and
most of the German Expressionists, he was not essentially
a social reformer. As O'Neill himself pointed out, the
crucial problem of his plays is not the individual's relationship to society, but rather the individual's relationship to some superior power, to God.

The critics shared Cook's enthusiasm for *The Emperor Jones*. His financial gamble on O'Neill's play paid
off in the Provincetowners' biggest success since the for-
mation of the company. In Europe the play was unfortunately handicapped by poor productions. In a Berlin
production in 1923 the emperor found himself impris-
oned in a virgin forest, which, according to one critic,
looked more like a city backyard hung with dirty wash-
ing than a jungle at night. A production at the Odéon
Theater in Paris the same year was even worse: here
Jones's attempt to escape from himself becomes a scram-
ble on all fours with his former subjects in hot pursuit.

However, there were fair European evaluations,
such as a short critical essay on O'Neill by Hugo von
Hofmannsthal, the Austrian poet and playwright, who
regarded *The Emperor Jones*, along with *Anna Christie*,
The First Man, and *The Hairy Ape*, as being "throughout essentially of the theater. Each play is clear-cut and
sharp in outline, solidly constructed from beginning to
end." Yet the conclusion of *The Emperor Jones*, like
that of *The Hairy Ape*, seemed to Hofmannsthal to be
"too direct, too simple, too expected; it is a little dis-

appointing to a European with his complex background, to see the arrow strike the target towards which he has watched it speeding all the while" (*The Freeman*, 21 March 1923).

In June 1921, *Gold* opened at the Frazee Theater in New York City. With *Beyond the Horizon, Anna Christie*, and *The Emperor Jones*, O'Neill had raised the standards of American drama, and the reviewers were now all the more critical of plays that failed to meet them. According to O'Neill, *Gold* was an earlier version of the one-act *Where the Cross Is Made*, although the latter was performed first. The four-act play is even less effective than the short one. *Gold* really does no more than add a tedious three-act prologue to a drama that had been compressed into one act, culminating in the scene with the flesh-and-blood ghosts. It lacks all dramatic tension until the last act, when the O'Neill of *The Emperor Jones* showed himself. The pathological illusion of Captain Bartlett that his wrecked ship will return with a cargo of treasure becomes so intense that even his son is carried away by it and begins to see the lights of the returning ship. The hallucination collapses when the captain glimpses the truth through his madness and kills his son. But this fourth act was not strong enough to save the play, and *Gold* closed after thirteen performances.

Failures always drove O'Neill to drink—although it must be said that he never needed the excuse of a failure. He was drinking intermittently, in spite of good resolutions and Prohibition. His friends still included plenty of people who would have been at home at

Jimmy the Priest's, and there was no lack of bootleg-
gers among them.

O'Neill's depression was increased by his failure to
find a producer for *The First Man*, but instead of fretting
over rejections he began to work on a new idea. A friend
from his seagoing days named Driscoll committed suicide, and O'Neill believed that it was because he felt
that he didn't belong anywhere. Driscoll became Yank
of *The Hairy Ape*, the bragging stoker with the strength
of a gorilla whose sudden awareness of not belonging is
a poignant moment in the play.

The success achieved by the Provincetowners with
The Emperor Jones was the begining of their disintegra-
tion. Not wanting to refuse their first chance to earn
money, some of the actors in *The Emperor Jones* accepted roles in the Broadway production (at the Sel-
wyn Theater), despite Cook's opposition to this. Feeling
that this threatened the principle on which his idealistic
experimental theater was founded, Cook believed that
the best thing for the Provincetown Players was an
abrupt death. Cook's withdrawal and the fact that
O'Neill was turning more and more toward the Broadway theater amounted in fact to a slow death for the
experimental company.

The production of *The Hairy Ape* proceeded without Jig Cook. O'Neill was soon involved in a new controversy, because some critics interpreted the play in a
manner he never intended. The audience could not overlook the fact that this play represented an unusual treatment of the evolution theory: Yank's obsessive search for
the place in which he belongs leads him to the gorilla's

cage. At first Yank seems convincing in his strength, his healthy animal physique, his brutal and successful claim to leadership of the other stokers. But his size and self-confidence are not what they seem. His philosophy is that men like him have mastered the world because they control machines and thus keep the world running, but it is reiterated so often that it loses all credibility for an audience of nonstokers. It is one of the lies lived by many of O'Neill's characters, and it collapses within seconds when Mildred Douglas, the daughter of a steel magnate, appears in the sooty stokehold, unreal in her white dress, and faints at the sight of Yank, black with coal dust and dripping with sweat.

Everything Yank believes is shattered, and his anger drives him to New York, to show Fifth Avenue society who belongs and who doesn't. But he cannot make contact with Fifth Avenue society. Their anonymous faces pass by like masks; these people are as incomprehensible to him in their invulnerability as spineless rubber puppets. The scene presents a situation typical of German Expressionist drama of the first two decades of the twentieth century: the alienation of the central figure in a dehumanized, hostile world. Yank's fear of not belonging drives him on, and he tries to enlist the help of the Industrial Workers of the World. They cannot understand him and throw him out. In the final scene, as he wanders through the zoo, he tries to communicate with a caged gorilla. Yank sees in the gorilla a kindred spirit—an unwanted, uncultured brute: "Ain't we both members of de same club—de Hairy Apes?" Yet when he frees the gorilla, he is killed by his fellow

"hairy ape." Yank's self-respect and sense of identity had
been obliterated by his exposure to Mildred, a member of a cultured elite, to which Yank could never belong. But neither does he belong on the animal level of
existence, free from conscience, self-awareness, social distinction, and feelings of inferiority. Just as he longed
for acceptance in the human world, he now longs for the
same in the naive innocence of the animal world. He is
caught between the two worlds, aware of both, but belonging to neither. "I ain't on oith and I ain't in heaven,
get me? I'm in de middle tryin' to separate 'em, takin'
all de woist punches from bot' of 'em. Maybe dat's what
dey call hell, huh?" Yank becomes a symbol of the human condition: the fusion of human and subhuman,
alone in an estranged world of indifference.

The Fifth Avenue scene presented some problems
during rehearsals, and one member of the company suggested giving the society faces a ghostly air of unreality
by using masks. This device of masks proved effective,
and O'Neill later admitted that he should have used
masks more extensively in *The Hairy Ape*. In "Second
Thoughts" (*The American Spectator*, December 1932)
he maintained that wider use of masks

would be of the greatest value in emphasizing the theme of the
play. From the opening of the fourth scene, where Yang begins
to think he enters into a masked world, even the familiar faces
of his mates in the forecastle have become strange and alien.
They should be masked, and the faces of everyone he encounters
thereafter, including the symbolic gorilla's.

Meanwhile rehearsals for *The First Man* were proceeding, and this play opened on 4 May 1922 at the

Neighborhood Playhouse but closed after twenty-seven performances. Both plot and action are lacking in imagination. Martha and Curtis Jayson, desolated by the death of their two children, have decided to remain childless and devote themselves to anthropological research. Over the years, however, Martha comes to realize that a woman's field is not scholarship but child care. She astonished her husband by announcing that she is pregnant. Curtis can see a baby only as an interloper who will interfere with his work. He refuses to acknowledge the child and in his hatred expresses the wish that it be stillborn. His attitude persuades their relatives, pillars of small-town society exaggerated to the point of caricaure, that the father of the child is not Curtis but his friend Bigelow. The play ends with Martha's death in childbirth and Curtis's remarkably tardy discovery of the family resentment.

In a sudden change of heart, for which little motivation is suggested, Curtis acknowledges the child, entrusts it to the care of a not very responsible aunt, and with a final tirade against the family leaves the house to catch the five-o'clock train on his way back to the habitat of "the first man." The couple's misunderstandings, Curtis's inability to interpret the town's hostility toward his wife, and his lame change of heart are psychologically so unconvincing that the play lacks credibility. Moreover, the proliferation of characters—eight family members—to provide a vehicle for the secondary theme of social criticism destroys its concentration. *The First Man* turned out to be a failure.

In February 1922 O'Neill's mother, who had been

staying with his brother in California while they disposed of James O'Neill's property there, suddenly died. Ella O'Neill had miraculously overcome her long narcotics addiction and became a cheerful, animated woman. She and her son Jamie had helped each other to resist their long-standing addictions—for Jamie had sworn off liquor. After his mother's death, however, he began to drink again and continued doing so until his early death. O'Neill's reactions to these events, which were made all the more distressing by the shipping of his mother's body to New York and Jamie's arrival in a state of drunken demoralization, are reflected in *A Moon for the Misbegotten*. Here he tried twenty years later to understand and to come to terms with some of his most harrying earlier experiences.

The Hairy Ape had been received with reserved applause, but as with *Anna Christie* several critics, among them Heywood Broun, misinterpreted it and mistook the play for propaganda for the Industrial Workers of the World. Once again O'Neill felt obliged to answer his critics, pointing out that *The Hairy Ape* was propaganda only in the sense that it symbolized man's loss of his old harmony with nature. "The struggle used to be with the gods," he said, "but is now with himself, his own past, his attempt to belong."

Inevitably some critics accused him of plagiarism or pointed to the influence of other writers. *The Hairy Ape* was said to show an undeniable parallel with Georg Kaiser's *The Coral* and with the *Gas* trilogy as a whole; and indeed the confrontation and contrasting of rich and poor in the third act of *The Hairy Ape* is very similar to that in the second act of *The Coral*. As has been pointed out, O'Neill was familiar with Kaiser's plays, but whether the similarities are accidental or not, the two writers were dealing with quite different problems. Yank, the central figure in *The Hairy Ape* (like Reuben Light in the later *Dynamo*), is not a victim of the machine like the factory hands in *Gas*. He is not a representative of the working class; he stands for man who in losing his relationship to God has lost his sense of belonging.

The Hairy Ape continued its run at the Plymouth Theater after a change of cast (first production on 17 April 1922). Mary Blair, who created the role of Mildred Douglas, was replaced by Carlotta Monterey. O'Neill's encounters with this beautiful actress were brief and not particularly friendly. He returned to Provincetown soon after the opening, little suspecting the role she was to play in his life.

In the fall of 1923 O'Neill agreed to write a new one-acter for George Jean Nathan's and H. L. Mencken's new *American Mercury*. But this play, *All God's Chillun Got Wings*, soon expanded into two acts. The protagonists, a young Negro boy and a white girl from the same neighborhood, are first shown in two early phases of their lives: a childhood scene when adult prejudices mean nothing to them or arouse at most a childish, idealistic resistance, followed by a scene in which prejudice results in their separation. After being thrown over by a brutal, loud-mouthed prizefighter, the girl overcomes her own inhibitions and marries her black childhood sweetheart. They go to France, but soon find it is no use running away and return to face the difficulties awaiting them. Their struggle to hold onto happiness is played out between emotional extremes of hatred, fear, and desperately clinging love, within the walls of a room that seems to be closing menacingly in upon them under the gaze of a secretly triumphant African mask. Their hope that help may come from outside—that the husband may eventually find recognition and a position as a lawyer —proves vain. When they are thrown back upon each other, their sense of failure is catastrophic, yet it bears within it the hopeful germ of a fresh start. The outcome, an unresolved question eliciting the sympathy of the audience, lies beyond the ending of the play.

Reports of the forthcoming production of *All God's Chillun Got Wings*, with Paul Robeson as Jim Harris, caused a storm of protest from segregationists. Conservative newspapers led the campaign and published warnings and protests by well-known figures in public life. They were particularly upset over the fact that a white actress would have to kiss a Negro's hand. Augustus Thomas, the highly paid writer of the commercial theater whom O'Neill so despised, participated in the campaign, speaking of "a tendency to break down social barriers which are better left untouched."

Once again O'Neill felt it necessary to defend his work.

The play itself, as anyone who has read it with intelligence knows, is never a "race problem" play. Its intention is confined to portraying the special lives of individual human beings. It is primarily a study of the two principal characters, and their tragic struggle for happiness. To deduce any general application from "God's Chillun" except in a deep, spiritual sense, is to read a meaning into my play which is not there, and I feel confident that even the most prejudiced could not fail to acknowledge this if they should see the play.

O'Neill's defense failed to halt the attack on the play, and the Ku Klux Klan now began to make threatening protests. At the premiere on 15 May 1924 the first scene had to be read in front of the curtain because the authorities had refused to issue an employment permit for juvenile actors. There were no riots but there were no good reviews, either. The play was too unsensational to live up to the exaggerated publicity.

It is interesting to note that in 1930 O'Neill attended a guest performance of *All God's Chillun Got Wings* by the Moscow Kamerny Theater at the Pigalle in Paris. The Russian director, Alexander Tairov, a great admirer of the American playwright, had renamed the play *Negro*, made a few "ideological" changes, and provided a number of technical innovations. For instance, emphasis on class feeling altered to some extent O'Neill's interpretation of race psychology. As to technical matters, Tairov increased the tension of big-city life through the use of the jarring sounds of New York's traffic, and in various ways accentuated the devices of Expressionism.

O'Neill approved the architectonic setting, the cinematographic techniques, and the rhythmic staging of his plays and found Tairov's interpretation of *All God's Chillun Got Wings* (and *Desire under the Elms*) very much to his liking. He was amazed to find that these productions rang true to the spirit of his work, that they had been conceived by Tairov "with that rarest of all gifts in a director—creative imagination! They were interpreted by . . . extraordinary artists . . . with that rarest of all gifts in actors and actresses— creative imagination again!" (*New York Herald Trib-une*, 19 June 1932). O'Neill, who always had reservations about the staging of his plays, felt that Tairov and his group of actors had realized his own concept of an imaginative theater.

5

Desire, Masks, and "Beautiful Philosophy"

These successful experiments in handling American themes in terms of Expressionist drama, which O'Neill knew from the works of Strindberg and Wedekind, and later Georg Kaiser and Ernst Toller, did not end O'Neill's search for new forms, and he began to explore the possibilities of "dramatized philosophy." But before this came the first performance of *Desire under the Elms* at the Greenwich Village Theater on 11 November 1924. Though the critics failed to discern the hallmark of a future American classic, the public seemed to think otherwise, and the play ran until October of the following year, moving from Greenwich Village to two Broadway theaters. It benefited from the same sort of publicity that had aroused such questionable interest in *All God's Chillun Got Wings*. O'Neill's friends were obliged to submit opinions by several eminent men (including, ironically enough, Augustus Thomas) to the New York authorities to prevent the play from being closed on the grounds of immorality. Finally a jury ruled that there was no case for banning *Desire under the Elms* or requiring any rewriting. But it was banned in Boston, and in Los Angeles the actors appearing in it were arrested.

In England *Desire under the Elms* was banned from public theaters on the vague grounds that it was "abhorrent." This decision was severely criticized in the British and American press, and the opinion was expressed that the banning of *Desire under the Elms* means a serious blow at the English theater: "It will put us back thirty years if plays by such dramatists as O'Neill are to be forbidden" (*The Observer*, 9 August

1925). After a private performance at the Gate Theatre in 1938, however, permission was finally granted for a regular production, and in 1940 it opened at the Westminster Theatre. Its reception soon dispelled the superficial criticisms the censors had made. Ivor Brown, for instance, said in his review in the *Illustrated London News* (10 February 1940) that *Desire under the Elms* had

the power of passion, the pulse of animalism, and with it a kind of poetical ground-well, as though underneath all the ugly happenings were some beauty fighting to emerge. Mr. O'Neill has written of humans who are as close to the farmyard in feeling and conduct as in economic fact, but he remembers that the farmyard is both the product and the cause of green fields. Out of, as well as into, its muck and mire come summer's loveliness and autumn's mellow fruitfulness.

The psychiatrist Philip Weissman made the interesting observation that *Desire under the Elms* is an "unconscious autobiography," and indeed O'Neill felt no scruples about portraying his father again in later plays, whether disguised as in *A Touch of the Poet* or openly as in *Long Day's Journey into Night*. Anyone familiar with these portraits will easily recognize Ephraim Cabot as Eugene's image of his father transposed into the dour world of a New England farm and the dramatic situation of the play. Ever since childhood Eben, the son, has been dominated and, as he believes, crushed by his father's harsh, intolerant philosophy of life and his belief in Old Testament inexorability. In an obvious parallel with *Long Day's Journey into Night* and *A Touch of the Poet*, Eben's resistance and hatred of his father are fomented by the belief that this philosophy was responsible for his mother's death, and he feels that this loss demands vengeance.

At the age of seventy-five Ephraim brings home a young bride, Abbie, who provides Eben with his opportunity of revenge, for she is attracted by his youth and vitality and knows that he will inherit the farm. Their love, at first no more than desire and a means to an end, grows to transcend its original bounds of hatred and scheming. The catastrophe precipitated when Eben accuses Abbie of using him merely to father a child and she kills the baby as a kind of catharsis in order to prove him wrong. Eben acknowledges his complicity in Abbie's deed and voluntarily goes with her to prison.

It may be true that O'Neill deliberately introduced Greek elements such as infanticide and incest into American drama, but what makes *Desire under the Elms* so compelling is the construction of plot and characters (especially that of Ephraim) and the stylistic sureness. It never suggests a montage; the tragic action is completely convincing. Several features recall Ibsen's *Rosmersholm*: the similar prehistories of Abbie and Rebecca; the symbols of the house representing all that is strong, old, and joyless; the bridge and the elms representing a dead woman whose spirit lives on, dominating the lives of Rosmer and Eben; and the attempts to break free of the past through an action in which love and death merge.

O'Neill was in Bermuda during the controversy over *Desire under the Elms*. The restlessness that drove him in his youth had not been allayed by intellectual work. Like Ella in *Long Day's Journey into Night*, he was always seeking a permanent home. Believing he had finally found it, he would buy and fix up houses at considerable expense, only to grow dissatisfied with them and move on. His marriage to Agnes Boulton had become a matter of habit. Agnes, who rated her own literary talents highly, had not accommodated herself to his needs and pursued a lively social life of her own.

In Bermuda, O'Neill finished *The Great God Brown*, in which, for the first time, he consistently exploited the potentialities of masks as a primary dramatic element. The two leading characters, Brown and Dion Anthony, are seen with and without masks, indicating the alternation between appearance and reality, between the conscious and the subconscious, between the external, social self and the hidden, true self. In Dion's case, these two manifestations become increasingly divergent, until—reaching the extremes of the blasphemous, demoralized cynic (represented by the mask) and the spiritual, ascetic mystic (his true self)— an unbearable tension arises, at which point Dion breaks down. The ultimate conflict in Dion's psychological makeup is reflected in his name: Dion=Dionysus, the mythological god associated with intoxication and ecstatic frenzy, representing primal forces of the subconscious mind. Anthony=St. Anthony, the monastic, represents rational, conscious control imposed upon basic human drives. Dion Anthony is an amalgamation of these antithetical psychological forces or states of being, a synthesis of Nietzsche's Apollonian

and Dionysian principles which underlie creative activity.

Brown, Dion's antagonist, who, like the main character in *Marco Millions*, exemplifies the empty successful
life of the materialist, lives in constant envy of Dion, the
sensitive artist in an unsympathetic, materialistic society. Dion's compulsive striving toward a creative life
and mystical fulfillment is beyond Brown's reach. The
rivalry between the two is revealed in their relationship to Margaret (Dion's wife and the object of
Brown's love), who, for O'Neill, is the "image of the
modern direct descendant of the Marguerite of *Faust*
—the eternal girl-woman with a virtuous simplicity of
instinct, properly oblivious to everything but the means
to her end of maintaining the race" ("The Playwright
Explains," *The New York Times*, 14 February 1926).
Dion is stronger than his rival. Finding solace in the
prostitute Cybel (a character reminiscent of Lulu in
Wedekind's *Earth Spirit* and Alice in Strindberg's *The
Dance of Death*), the Mother Earth figure who pos-
sesses a wisdom of, and naïve confidence in, life, Dion
inspires the construction plans of the architect Brown.
Although slowly consuming himself, Dion remains un-
reachable for his materially successful rival. Upon
Dion's death, Brown, thinking he has acquired Dion's
creative power, takes his mask and thus assumes Dion's
identity, both as Margaret's husband and as the re-
cipient of Cybel's consolation.

The Nietzschean overtones of this transfiguration
of Dion into Brown—"Dion Brown," as Cybel calls him
—are enhanced by Brown's remarks immediately after
he puts on Dion's mask: "Welcome, dumb worship-

pers! I am your Great God Brown! I have been advised to run from you but it is my almighty whim to dance into escape over your prostrate souls!" In assuming Dion's identity, Brown has become the god Dionysus, dancing among his reveling followers. When Brown is mistakenly shot by police, his last words echo Nietzsche's *The Birth of Tragedy*:

"Blessed are they that weep, for they shall laugh!" Only he that has wept can laugh! The laughter of Heaven sows earth with a rain of tears, and out of Earth's transfigured birth-pain the laughter of Man returns to bless and play again in innumerable dancing gales of flame upon the knees of God!

The play concludes with the suggestion of Nietzsche's theme of the "eternal return," when the epilogue, presenting Margaret and her three sons four years later, takes place, like the prologue, at a dance on the pier of the casino. Beginning a new cycle in the recurrence of human events, the boys are told to "go in and dance," while Margaret, alone with Dion's mask, evokes the eternal Dionysian spirit of her departed husband.

In the light of the difficulties audiences and readers encountered in coming to terms with *The Great God Brown* intellectually, O'Neill felt compelled to interpret the symbolism of the play and its meaning, at least as far as he wished "an audience to comprehend it." Ultimately, he maintains in "The Playwright Explains" that it is "Mystery—the mystery any one man or woman can feel but not understand as the meaning of any event—or accident—in any life on earth. And it is this mystery I want to realize in the theater."

O'Neill soon returned to New York to attend re-

hearsals of *The Fountain*, the first in a series of unusually long plays. He had begun with one-acters cen-
tered on a moment in time, which forcefully presented
an idea or a disclosure in an atmosphere of great concentration. His first attempt at a longer play, *Beyond
the Horizon*, had been rewarded with the Pulitzer
Prize. He now began to give more rein to his imagination, continued to experiment, and became more confident in his power of expression. But while some of his
later plays managed to hold the audience's attention
for hours, *The Fountain* did not. The familiar story of
Ponce de Leon's search for the fountain of eternal
youth and the play's message—that youth is to be found
only within man's soul—are straightforward and trans-
parent, but O'Neill did not succeed in enhancing the
idea with poetic beauty or working it out into a logical
sequence of actions. The austere language sometimes
seems inappropriate. Above all, the play is too long
to sustain interest in a more or less undeveloped idea.
It was two years before *The Fountain* was produced,
and by this time O'Neill was far enough away from it
not to be unduly upset at the poor reception it received.

Moreover, he was now absorbed in *The Great God
Brown*, which opened on 23 January 1926 at the Greenwich Village Theater. The critics' reaction was a mix-
ture of intellectual confusion and general admiration
for the play's dramatic qualities. The effectiveness of
the masks was impaired by uncertainty about their
function; to some critics they were no more than a bor-
ing trick, to others they represented an interesting ex-

periment. According to Joseph Wood Krutch (*The Nation*, 10 February 1926):

At no time during the course of his career has Mr. O'Neill given us a play more powerful or more confused than this. . . . If the effect remains more powerful than clear, more intense than illuminating, that is the result of the immediacy of the material with which the author is dealing. . . . Here, in a word, are passions as authentic and as burning as any that ever went into literature, but no one could say that they had been "recollected in tranquillity."

Even after the failure of this "trick" O'Neill continued to believe that it was the use of half-masks that had lessened the impact of his theme. They had accentuated the well-known fact that man masks his face when he confronts his fellow man but not the mystical idea on which the play was based. But it is questionable whether his theme could have been clearly expressed, even with masks twice the size of those actually used.

O'Neill pursued the idea of using masks for many years. In 1932 he published an essay entitled "Memoranda on Masks" (*The American Spectator*, November 1932), in which he asserted that masks were a suitable device for the modern drama which must inevitably emerge in the future and eventually become

the freest solution of the modern dramatist's problem as to how —with the greatest possible dramatic clarity and economy of means—he can express those profound hidden conflicts of the mind which the probings of psychology continue to disclose to us. He must find some method to present this inner drama in his work, or confess himself incapable of portraying one of the most characteristic preoccupations and uniquely significant, spiritual impulses of his time.

O'Neill contrasted the mask with "a realistically disguised surface symbolism" which, to O'Neill, is as shallow as it is misleading.

A comprehensive expression is demanded here, a chance for eloquent presentation, a new form of drama projected from a fresh insight into the inner forces motivating the actions and reactions of men and women . . . , a drama of souls, and the adventures of "free wills," with the masks that govern them and constitute their fates.

With specific reference to the actors, O'Neill had this to say:

Looked at from even the most practical standpoint of the practicing playwright, the mask *is* dramatic in itself, *has always* been dramatic in itself, *is* a proven weapon of attack. At its best, it is more subtly, imaginatively, suggestively dramatic than any actor's face can ever be.

Anticipating the objections of the actors to the use of masks, O'Neill claimed that "masks would give them the opportunity for a totally new kind of acting, that they would learn many undeveloped possibilities of their art . . . ," and concluded that "masks did not extinguish the Greek actor, nor have they kept the acting of the East from being an art" ("A Dramatist's Notebook," *The American Spectator*, January 1933). Behind this attitude of course lay his distrust of actors who took it upon themselves to give their own interpretation of a role. James O'Neill's son was suspicious of actors and personally supervised rehearsals of many of his plays, so it is not surprising that he should have regarded the mask as another means of restraining the actor's disturbing individuality. Moreover, this theory

of masks is obviously an attempt to rationalize and
profit by the success of *The Great God Brown*, although
his repeated references to its success are not entirely
justified, since for many critics and members of the
public the masks themselves had lessened the play's
impact. While the idea of using masks in crowd scenes
to create a feeling of impersonal, collective mass psychology may have been worth trying out, as O'Neill
did in *The Hairy Ape*, *The Great God Brown* proved
that the realistic devices of a dramatist like Ibsen—
facial expression, gesture, and above all the spoken
word—can express much more sophisticated and subtle
dramatic effects than can be achieved with masks.
O'Neill's reference to Japanese Noh plays has little
relevance to the problems he dealt with, and whenever
he went in for mystical philosophy he found himself
beyond the range of his experience and encountered
some difficulty in expressing himself. In later plays he
made no use of actual masks. Like many of his "phi-
losophies," this one too was short-lived.

O'Neill returned to Bermuda after discussions with
the great Broadway showman David Belasco regarding a production of his marathon play *Marco Millions*
had reached a stalemate. Apparently the discrepancy
between this play's chances of success and what it
would cost to produce it deterred even a showman like
Belasco. In a letter to him O'Neill had mentioned the
play's disadvantages, its length and elaborate settings,
but at the same time he stressed its "beauty and philosophy," as well as the fact that this was a satirical
comedy written by an American about the life and

ideals of Americans, that is to say, of materialists who
seek money in preference to beauty and truth. The old
theme is developed in scenes from the life of an
Americanized Marco Polo as he is transformed from
an amorous dreamer into a vainglorious materialist. This
play, like *Lazarus Laughed*, illustrates a talent in which
O'Neill had few equals: his ability to use actors, stage
properties, music, and other like elements on an extraordinarily lavish scale without falling into extravagance.
This is quite characteristic of his stagecraft, as is his
use of color: the costumes in *Mourning Becomes Electra*, for instance, which immediately suggest gloom,
or the contrast of the snow-white dress of the million-
aire's daughter with the sooty stokehole in *The Hairy
Ape*. Here the colors almost have the impact of words.
O'Neill's love of painting is particularly evident in
Marco Millions (as well as in *Lazarus Laughed*). The
set becomes a densely crowded canvas on which he
tries, not unsuccessfully, to paint his idea of the fascinating, un-American Orient. But this talent is ac-
complished by the weakness that mars *Marco Millions* as it mars *Lazarus Laughed* and *Strange Interlude*:
O'Neill's notorious repetitiousness and prolixity. This
is more apparent when one reads the plays, and if the
tempo of the performance is at certain times stepped
up, as it was in Heinz Hilpert's production of *Strange
Interlude* in Berlin in 1929, the repetitiousness can produce an effectively persistent rhythm. This is especially
true of *The Iceman Cometh*.

So far as "beautiful philosophy" is concerned,
Marco Millions is open to severe criticism. The drama-

tization of Eastern mentalities amounts to little more than a cliché of the contemplative Orient, while Marco is the stereotype of the soulless, commercial West. This is not criticism of American culture so much as mere statement of commonplaces. On the other hand the interplay of characters—Marco, Kublai, and Princess Kukachin—against a panoramic background of the time well repaid the effort O'Neill put into it—although the whole thing sometimes seems uncomfortably close to Cecil B. De Mille.

The rejection of *Marco Millions* by David Belasco and Max Reinhardt did not deter O'Neill from writing another equally elaborate play: *Lazarus Laughed* (first published in 1927). This too contains some "beautiful philosophy" and O'Neill cannot refrain from dinning it into the audience's ear. Observations such as "There is no death" and "Death is dead" are repeated *ad infinitum*. As so often happens when he becomes too philosophical, he exceeds the limits of dramatic good sense. Lazarus, raised from the dead by Jesus, shocks his family and fellow citizens by what he has learned in death: that man's life is dominated by fear of death, that his salvation lies in realizing that life does not die, that life is laughter. Lazarus goes to Greece, then to Rome. The infectious, melodious sound of his laughter pervades the play, bringing an irresistible momentary whiff of possible salvation into the lives of all those he encounters—people who are on their guard against death and kill from fear of it. O'Neill had made a study of Bergson's treatise on laughter and Freud's *Wit and Its Relation to the Un-*

conscious. He found Bergson's theory too mechanistic and Freud's too erotic, and thought that both missed the essential point: that laughter is an unexplainable emotional overflowing.

But *Lazarus Laughed* is also repetitious. It is impossible for the laughter to be as melodic and varied throughout this lengthy play as the stage directions demand. It is also unlikely that O'Neill's idea of suggesting crowds by using masks depicting all human categories would have worked out in practice. Nonetheless, the directors' premature rejection of the play as unstageable seems unjustified. *Lazarus Laughed* has never been put to the test of a production that followed O'Neill's stage directions. Irritated and persistent, he did everything he could to get it produced—he even went so far as to suggest that Feodor Chaliapin play the leading role in Russian—but he had to be content with an amateur performance in Pasadena, California, in 1928.

6

Modern "Tragedy"

O'Neill's domestic situation had become precarious after meeting the actress Carlotta Monterey again in 1927 and establishing a close friendship with her. He had not yet found a permanent home, although he had bought and restored an eighteenth-century house in Bermuda and owned a summer cottage in Maine. To him Carlotta Monterey personified the sophisticated, self-reliant woman, whose talent for organization and sympathetic attitude he contrasted with Agnes's instability and superficial sociability.

Believing that the time had come for the Theater Guild to present O'Neill, Lawrence Langner, its director, went to see him in Bermuda. The Guild had been founded in 1919, after the Provincetown Players and the Washington Square Theater, and provided additional scope for the rising generation of American dramatists. In April 1925 it had acquired its own theater in New York and regularly presented plays by younger American writers. O'Neill's association with the Theater Guild proved extraordinarily productive, and many of his later plays were first performed by this company. After some difficulties he induced its sponsors and directors to accept both *Marco Millions* and his recently finished *Strange Interlude*, and in November 1927 he left Bermuda to attend rehearsals of both plays in New York. The limited resources of the Guild forced him to make radical cuts and changes in *Marco Millions*. During the rehearsal period O'Neill devoted most of his attention to *Strange Interlude*, probably because he always considered his latest play his best, but also because he was aware of the enormous risk he was taking with this play. For one thing, the characters' asides, comparable to interior monologues, defy dramatic principles by blurring the line of demarcation between drama and novel. Moreover, the play is unusually long; it lasts five hours and makes extraordinary demands on the audience. Besides following the plot they must also try to follow the dialogue on two levels, taking in both the relatively dissembling normal dialogue and the nondissembling stream-of-consciousness dialogue or monologue. In fact O'Neill was now doing through speech what he had tried to do through masks. One would think that this device would work best in a one-act play, but in his experimentation O'Neill gave little consideration to his audience or to his actors.

The heroine Nina Leeds leaves her father's house after her aviator fiancé has been shot down in World War I, accusing her father of having prevented her from consummating her love. To atone for her own guilt she offers servicemen in a military hospital what she had withheld from Gordon. In order to give her life some meaning she marries Sam, a good-natured, honest, hard-working but not particularly intelligent college friend of Gordon's. She is not in love with him, but hopes that having children may normalize her life. This hope is shattered when her mother-in-law tells her that her husband, like his father, is in danger of becoming insane. In order to fulfill her marriage with Sam, Nina commits adultery with Ned Darrell, a doctor friend of the family, but her scheme gets out of hand when she falls in love with the father of her child. From now on she lives out the triple role of mother, wife, and mistress. This is the portrait of a possessive woman who has succeeded in acquiring, at least for a time, everything her feminine nature craves: a husband and father (Sam), a lover (Ned), a son (Gordon), and a father figure (Charlie Marsden), an effete novelist afflicted with an Oedipus complex. It is not surprising that O'Neill found conventional dramatic techniques inadequate to deal with so complex a character as Nina. Her dream collapses: her son marries; her lover leaves her to devote himself to his work; Sam stagnates in complacency. Nina fights in vain to hold on to her "possessions," but finds herself worn out, defeated and helpless. A life of "contented weariness" with Charlie Marsden is all that remains to her.

Strange Interlude derives its vitality from several levels of meaning. The life styles of the three men, Charlie's superficial "poeticizing" of reality, Ned's rational diagnosis of life, and Sam's materialistic happiness, are all inadequate for realizing a total vision of life. None of them fully understands Nina as a woman or arouses all the love she is capable of. These are symptoms of what O'Neill saw as "the sickness of today." This fragmentation into separate, unrelated attitudes is exactly what Nina thought she could overcome by loving three men. Obviously, all this arises from a characteristic O'Neill depth psychology. Although the character of Nina Leeds is somewhat overdrawn, O'Neill succeeds, through the use of the asides, in presenting a dual image of her, and thus reveals an added dimension of "Everywoman." The principal merit of this play lies not in its criticism of the age, its psychological revelations or its complex portrait of a woman, but in the skillfully narrated story, which ends, in spite of the occasionally tiresome two-level structure, in a dramatically and humanly credible solution.

Fears that critics and public would dismiss *Strange Interlude* as outrageous proved excessively pessimistic. Although a few New York newspapers did attack the play, the majority of critics felt, with some reservations, that the experiment was a success, and the public gave it a vote of confidence unique in O'Neill's career. It closed after 414 performances and continued its triumphant run on tour and as a motion picture. It won O'Neill his third Pulitzer Prize and became the subject of several serious literary studies.

In Berlin, *Strange Interlude*, with Elisabeth Bergner in the leading role, became a somewhat controversial success. Its length and its affinity to Ibsen were held against it, but Elisabeth Bergner scored a personal triumph as Nina. It was this role that made the deepest impression on many critics; its complexity and depth are an almost inexhaustible challenge to any actress, and Miss Bergner rose to this challenge. Her triumphant performance elicited such laudatory comments as Fritz Engel's (*Berliner Tageblatt* of 5 November 1929):

A brown-haired, troubled, sick girl, then a young mother who should not be one, then a lovely woman, then again a mother, then fading charms under a red wig, then an elderly lady, then a gentle old woman, and much more in the intervals—nine acts, nine roles, nine times a woman's love, suffering and hate-driven and driving through disillusionments and ecstasies; nine times the same person and yet another person, and always herself, with those eyes which do not need O'Neill's trick devices to say what must not be said; always with that child's face which can suddenly become tragic; always with that lovely charm which spreads a welcome cheerfulness; . . . it is Eve triumphant. We are willing to pardon O'Neill much. He gives occasion for great art in acting.

Early in 1928 O'Neill left the United States for Europe with Carlotta Monterey. It had been agreed that his wife would seek a divorce during his absence. After brief stays in London and Paris they rented a villa near Guéthary in the French Pyrenees. O'Neill kept his whereabouts a secret, and only a few friends were aware that he was not in California. In Guéthary he wrote the draft of a play he had had in mind for years: *Dynamo*, which he called "a symbolical and factual biography of what is happening in a large section of the American soul right now. It is really the first play of a trilogy that will dig at the roots of the sickness of today as I feel it." Nevertheless the play, with its unconvincing characters and turbid mysticism centering on a dynamo, failed to please either the critics or the public. O'Neill was obviously trying to deal with modern man's inclination toward "industrial religiosity," but his exaggeration and excessive elaboration of the theme appeared ridiculous, although not without dramatic effect. Reuben Light, the central character of *Dynamo*, rejects the values of his clergyman father and renounces God in favor of a theology of electricity. God is the energy of electric current. Through this God, Reuben seeks salvation and finds only, as the play ends, a macabre mystical union in which he immolates himself on the altar of his divinity, electrocuted by a dynamo. *Dynamo* was presented by the Theater Guild at the Martin Beck Theater on 11 February 1929, but closed after a few performances. O'Neill himself soon developed a dislike for the play, and finally admitted that the critics had been right and that "*Dynamo* doesn't count."

O'Neill's steadily increasing bitterness over Agnes's reluctance to grant him a divorce began to affect his work and his relationship with Carlotta. He decided to fulfill his dream of a voyage to East Asia, cherished since the days of *Beyond the Horizon* and *Marco Millions*. While rehearsals of *Dynamo* were proceeding in New York, he and Carlotta left France. But O'Neill's enthusiasm soon waned, and the trip that had been intended to last a year was over in four months, after visits to Saigon, Singapore, Manila, and Hong Kong. When reporters began to pursue him, O'Neill, disgusted with the publicity in the American press, changed his plans and returned to France, where he rented Le Plessis, a chateau near Tours. In July 1929 he and Carlotta were married in Paris, after Agnes Boulton had been granted her divorce in Reno. Marriage changed O'Neill's way of life and his relationship with a number of his friends. Carlotta was determined to organize his life so that nothing should interfere with his work. Isolated from his friends from his early Provincetown days, he lived in ever greater seclusion until his death.

At Le Plessis, Carlotta saw to it that he could work undisturbed on his most ambitious work to date, the trilogy *Mourning Becomes Electra*. Once finished, it was sent to the Theater Guild and immediately accepted, and O'Neill decided to go to New York for rehearsals. The original idea of spreading the trilogy over three successive evenings was abandoned. After the surprising success of *Strange Interlude*, the directors of the Guild did not hesitate to make demands on the audience's endurance. As a result, *Mourning Becomes Electra* was performed in a single evening, with intermissions after the first and second parts. This production lasted from five o'clock in the afternoon until midnight.

As early as 1926 O'Neill had written in his diary: "Modern psychological drama using one of the old legend plots of Greek tragedy—the story of Electra—Medea? Would it be possible to get a modern psychological approximation of the Greek sense of fate into this sort of play?" He went on to ask himself whether a modern audience, possessing no belief in gods or in supernatural retribution, "could accept and be moved" by such a play. In his diary, O'Neill makes frequent references to his intention of writing a "modern" version of the saga of the House of Atreus. Yet at no point in *Mourning Becomes Electra* is the parallel to the *Oresteia* of Aeschylus overstressed. As it is indicated by the numerous departures from the original legend, O'Neill never intended to create a meaningless vehicle merely for the purpose of retelling an ancient story, of providing a "historical-mythological dimension."

The first part of the trilogy, *Homecoming*, opens as the Mannon household awaits the victorious return of General Ezra Mannon from the Civil War. His wife, Christine, who is having an affair with a Captain Brant, and his daughter Lavinia, who knows about her mother's infidelity, hate each other. When the general returns, Christine, plotting with Brant, poisons him. In *The Hunted*, Lavinia's brother Orin returns home, and Lavinia sets a trap for Christine to convince him of their mother's guilt and the necessity of getting rid of her accomplice Brant, who has dishonored the family. Orin kills him, but leaves it up to Lavinia to tell their mother that vengeance has been done. Driven by guilt and a sense of persecution, Christine commits suicide.

In the third part, *The Haunted*, the two surviving Mannons, Lavinia and Orin, are drawn together in a climate of guilt and incest. Lavinia's incestuous love for her father is gradually transferred to her brother, so that she comes to assume her mother's place—a process which is indicated by her increasing physical resemblance to Christine. Orin loves his sister, as he loved Christine, as a woman, and their lives are now inexorably dominated by their sense of guilt. A voyage to the South Seas fails to liberate them from the past. Orin, too weak to carry this burden, commits suicide, leaving Lavinia to bear the guilt of the Mannons alone. The trilogy ends with her final renunciation of a happy life. Bound forever to the Mannon dead, Lavinia enters the house, whose shutters will now be nailed close, and shuts the door behind her.

In *Mourning Becomes Electra*, O'Neill uses characters as economically as in *Strange Interlude* without in any way diminishing the impact of the play. This is in complete contrast to *Lazarus Laughed* and *Marco Millions*, where an incomparable larger cast was needed to express the universality of the theme. While the plot is recognizable as that of the *Oresteia*, despite the many divergences, the intellectual parallels are tenuous. The concept of fate that O'Neill presents here is not that of Aeschylus. In the *Oresteia*, fate is called to life again with every deed and ends with its expiation. The doer of the deed determines his fate. He may have been forced into a fateful decision, but he bears the responsibility for it. The chain of fate can be broken with every new decision.

In O'Neill's trilogy, on the contrary, "fate" is an all-pervading condition, a disease whose advance manifests itself in the actions of the characters. Like Ibsen's *Ghosts,* O'Neill's trilogy is permeated by a continual reenactment of the past. But while Ibsen's characters are haunted by the "ghosts" of heredity, O'Neill's characters are victimized by a family curse arising from hatred, a psychological fixation rather than a physiological condition, from which they cannot escape. O'Neill's determinism, in this case, manifests itself as the Freudian sexual instinct and Oedipus complex.

Nevertheless, in both cases the ancient Greek concept of fate has been replaced by naturalistic determinism. *Mourning Becomes Electra*, which O'Neill later viewed "solely as a psychological play, quite removed from the confusing preoccupations the classical derivation of its plot once caused me" ("Memoranda on Masks"), is not so much a modernized *Oresteia* as a New England *Rosmersholm.*

Its affinities with Elizabethan tragedy, which O'Neill never mentions, go deeper, and a comparison with *Hamlet* in particular reveals many important parallels. The closet scene in *Hamlet* might almost be called archetypal for O'Neill's plot structure for the trilogy, which can be interpreted as a series of progressively violent duels. Christine is closer to Gertrude than to Clytaemnestra. While Clytaemnestra deliberately plans her actions, Christine seems to be compulsively driven to hers. In her relationship with Hazel, Orin's fiancée, she sometimes shows a reminiscent yearning that echoes Gertrude's recollections of her own youth reflected in Ophelia. The truth is brought home to both Orin and Hamlet through a trap. In both plays retribution is long delayed in a conflict between two irreconcilable characters: Claudius and Hamlet, Christine and Lavinia. Other parallels could be cited, such as the "antiromantic" cynicism that Hamlet and Orin have in common. Lavinia and Orin are the descendants of Hamlet, not of Orestes. Similarly, the citizens in O'Neill's trilogy serve not as the chorus of elders of ancient Greek tragedy, but as the commoners of Shakespearean tragedy.

Unanimously favorable reviews followed the premiere of *Mourning Becomes Electra* on 26 October 1931, and some critics considered it O'Neill's masterpiece. O'Neill was well on his way to establishing a reputation abroad, and out of all of his works up to this time, *Mourning Becomes Electra* contributed most toward winning for O'Neill the attention of a wide international public.

7

Christian Salvation and Redemption into Nothingness

O'Neill abandoned his original intention of returning to Le Plessis after the opening of *Mourning Becomes Electra*. Instead he built a Spanish villa in Georgia, and Carlotta furnished it at considerable expense. After they had moved into this latest "permanent home," Casa Genotta, O'Neill began the first of several drafts of the play which, after many false starts, changes, and, no doubt, many crises of conscience, finally became *Days without End*. But he set this work temporarily aside because, as he later explained, one night in September 1932 he dreamed a comedy, which he wrote down the next day at a single sitting. After six weeks of work he found himself with *Ah, Wilderness!*, a play far superior to *Days without End*, written in a fraction of the time the latter took him. Its subtitle, "a comedy of recollection," suggests an autobiographical element, which O'Neill acknowledged, although he pointed out that *Ah, Wilderness!* portrayed his youth as he would have liked it to have been.

Not surprisingly, many critics found O'Neill's plays lacking in humor. It was, after all, tragedy that had earned him his Broadway reputation. Yet if we look through his works for traces of humor we have to revise the image of a humorless O'Neill. Behind the serious seamen of the early sea plays, Chris in *Anna Christie*, or some of the characters in *The Iceman Cometh*, we sense an aloofly smiling author. One of his early plays, *The Movie Man*, was a tolerant satire on Latin American revolutionary enthusiasm and North American business acumen in which an American film company directs a Mexican revolution on the basis of camera angles and the tastes of the American movie-goer. Be that as it may, *Ah, Wilderness!* is the only comedy of O'Neill's maturity, and it shows a mastery that a newcomer to the field of humor could never have attained. Free from all pretentiousness, its concise, concentrated plot follows the young Richard Miller through the phases of his first love affair and his rebellion against established authority. This "comedy of recollection" relies less on situation than on treatment of characters. The comic situations of *Ah, Wilderness!* are merely a vehicle through which characters can express their universality. By concentrating on characterization, O'Neill avoided the stereotypes of conventional comedy, and created characters that are completely lifelike, nonabstract individuals, "energized" by memory.

The Theater Guild decided to produce *Ah, Wilderness!* before *Days without End*, probably out of fear the latter could never live up to the last O'Neill play that they had sponsored, *Mourning Becomes Electra*. After an out-of-town tryout in Pittsburgh, *Ah, Wilderness!* opened at the Guild Theater on 2 October 1933. As was to be expected, O'Neill's departure from serious drama came as a surprise. A few critics regarded it as a lapse into sentimental comedy, but Brooks Atkinson wrote in *The New York Times* of 3 October 1933 that "O'Neill has a capacity for tenderness that most of us never suspected. . . . Mr. O'Neill's point of view is full of compassionate understanding. . . . And in spite of its dreadful title, *Ah, Wilderness!* is a true and congenial comedy."

Days without End (1934), too, was given an out-of-town tryout, this time in Boston, where it received

moderately favorable reviews. But this was no guarantee
of success on Broadway. Boston, with its preponder-
antly Catholic population, was no place to test audience reaction to a Catholic confessional play such as
Days without End. Apart from some, though by no
means all, of the Catholic journals, the New York critics shared Brooks Atkinson's astonishment that O'Neill's
career could be so "uneven." Three extreme critical reactions illustrate how *Days without End* destroyed
O'Neill's image as a revolutionary young dramatist
ready to overthrow all conventions, dramatic as well
as idealistic. In the London *Observer* of 7 October
1934, St. John Ervine approved of the spirit of the
play:

The bitterness, the sophomoric cynicism, the subjection of intellect to undisciplined emotion, the animal brutality, and the
terrible hatred which defiled many of the plays up to and including *Mourning Becomes Electra* have almost disappeared or been
reduced to proper proportions. A sense of human dignity under
ordeal appears at last in Mr. O'Neill's mind, and the poet who
revealed himself in *Beyond the Horizon*, but has been hidden
ever since, is showing his head.

Ervine considers the defects of *Days without End*
"almost a testimonial to its virtues" and concludes that
the author of this play is "a new Mr. O'Neill, or
rather the old Mr. O'Neill absolved from his obsession."
The German critic Kurt Hohoff hailed O'Neill's "con-
version," saying that the yearnings faintly discernible
in plays such as *The Hairy Ape* and *The Great God
Brown* had now emerged as a firm, radiant faith
(*Hochland*, October 1938).

A. Abramov, on the other hand, wrote, in a Moscow review notable for its tone of harsh contempt, that "O'Neill has shown us his true face: the face of a churchman and obscurantist who has found his life's ideal in the garb of the Catholic priest. . . . He has said his last word" (*Literaturnaia Gazeta*, 12 December 1934).

It is not difficult to understand the predominantly unfavorable American reviews. O'Neill's "confessional play" does not reflect his ultimate position, neither does it present convincingly John Loving's "redemption" from the spirit of negation. Here O'Neill has reverted to the theme of spiritual conflict. John, the god-seeker, is constantly accompanied by Loving, the cynical nihilist, who counters his every impulse to yield to God and a belief in love and purity with the argument that everything passes and death heals all. It is not clear why O'Neill, who had proved his ability to reveal inner conflict through his characters' own words and actions, now resorted to the device of a devil's advocate slinking about behind John. In any case, this figure becomes unnecessary when John's own speeches begin to reflect his struggle. The simplistic nature of the device becomes painfully obvious in the closing scene, when John, prostrating himself before a crucifix, "mystically" experiences God, and Loving falls to the ground dead. O'Neill's retort had distilled nothing but a *homo dei* for whom the devil, temptation and negation were non-existent. In O'Neill psychology, such a creature could have no great life expectancy. Once again, O'Neill had fallen victim to his urge for dramatic clarity, which this time had evaporated in a simplistic prefabricated philosophy.

In the autumn of 1934, O'Neill began work on *A Tale of Possessors Self-Dispossessed*, a projected cycle of plays spanning a period of almost one hundred years, and drew up a detailed genealogy of the Harford family, on which the cycle was to be based. But its scope continued to expand, and O'Neill's obsession with epic completeness led him to reach increasingly farther back into the past of the main characters and their forefathers. However, *A Touch of the Poet* and *More Stately Mansions* are the only two plays that survive of the cycle.

In November 1936, O'Neill was in Seattle in search of atmosphere and detail for his new cycle when he was informed that he had been awarded the Nobel Prize for Literature. He had been a candidate before, but had been passed over in favor of Thomas Mann and Sinclair Lewis. Lewis had said in his acceptance speech (in 1930):

And had you chosen Mr. O'Neill who has done nothing much in American drama save to transform it utterly in ten or twelve years from a false world of neat and competent trickery to a world of splendor and fear and greatness, you would have been reminded that he has done something far worse than scoffing— he has seen life as not to be neatly arranged in the study of a scholar but as a terrifying, magnificent, and often quite horrible thing akin to the tornado, the earthquake and the devastating fire.

When O'Neill was chosen for the prize, he was ill and unable to attend the ceremonies in Stockholm. His acceptance speech had to be read for him. In it, reiterating his 1924 reference to Strindberg as "the forerunner of everything modern in the theater of today" (*Provincetown Playbill*, 3 January 1924), he paid tribute to the Swedish playwright as his model and his most decisive influence:

It was reading his plays when I first started to write back in the winter of 1913–14 that, above all else, first gave me the vision of what modern drama could be, and first inspired me with the urge to write for the theater myself. If there is anything of lasting worth in my work, it is due to that original impulse from him, which has continued as my inspiration down all the years since then—to the ambition I received then to follow in the footsteps of his genius as worthily as my talent might permit, and with the same integrity of purpose. . . . I am only too proud of my debt to Strindberg, only too happy to have this opportunity of proclaiming it to his people. For me, he remains, as Nietzsche remains in his sphere, the Master, still to this day more modern than any of us, still our leader. [*Nobel Lectures Literature, 1901–1967*, 1969, p. 337.]

O'Neill's debt to Strindberg has been accepted by most critics without question; nevertheless, it would seem that O'Neill owes less to him than to Ibsen. To be sure, the themes and techniques of many of the early plays show Strindberg's influence: the dramatic monologue in *Before Breakfast*, for instance, which recalls *The Stronger*, or the visions of the Emperor Jones, which may have been inspired by *To Damascus*. There are also traces in *All God's Chillun Got Wings*, *Welded*, and *Strange Interlude* of Strindberg's antifeminism and his idea that marriage embodies the antagonism between the sexes. That, however, is the extent of his literary influence. O'Neill seems to have been much more deeply affected by Strindberg the man, as he appears in his autobiographical writings, than by Strindberg the playwright. Ibsen actually had a more formative influence on him, and the parallels with his work are more numerous and significant, especially the parallel between Ibsen's "life-sustaining lie" and O'Neill's "pipe dreams" and the similarity of their denouement technique (these parallels can be seen in *The Iceman Cometh*). O'Neill's own statements about models and influences are often misleading, as has been seen in the case of Georg Kaiser.

The award of the Nobel Prize medal and citation was made in the Merritt Hospital in San Francisco, where O'Neill was recovering from an attack of appendicitis. This was followed by kidney complications, which marked the onset of a physical degeneration diagnosed (falsely, as it later appeared) as Parkinson's disease. The tremor in his hands which he had inherited from his mother (see *Long Day's Journey into Night*) increased. His handwriting grew smaller as he tried more and more desperately to control his hands, and his later attempts to switch to the typewriter or dictation were unsuccessful.

The O'Neills had given up Casa Genotta and were building a new house in California, a pseudo-Chinese one called Tao House, which was to be their last attempt to find a permanent home. After leaving the hospital, O'Neill resumed work on his play cycle. He finished *A Touch of the Poet* and wrote drafts for several more plays but refused to let any of them be produced before the complete cycle was finished. However, the strain of keeping in mind the plot details of these plays spanning a period of a hundred years without losing sight of their overall unity proved too much for him. He felt obliged to make constant changes, and every new change meant revising the drafts of the projected plays. By 1938 he had reached a point where it seemed advisable to set the cycle temporarily aside. As in the case of *Ah, Wilderness!*, the idea for a different play had been germinating in his mind and was now ready to be written.

In this play, *The Iceman Cometh*, O'Neill reverted once more to the past, to his New York days at Jimmy the Priest's. The action takes place in a shabby saloon somewhere in midtown New York in the year 1912. In this gloomy atmosphere, O'Neill assembles a group of seedy characters most of whom have given up any occupation they ever had and abandoned themselves to drink and their wishful illusions. Like Ibsen, especially in his *The Wild Duck*, O'Neill presents the human condition as such that man cannot live without clinging to some illusion or "life-lie." About a dozen of his characters are sprawled out on the iron chairs or asleep with their heads on the grimy tables. From time to time they ask the proprietor, an equally sorry character named Harry Hope, to stand them a drink. They are all waiting for Hickey, a hardware salesman who drops in once a year to celebrate Harry's birthday. But the Hickey who shows up this time is not the familiar old joker who regales them with lusty stories of his wife and the iceman. He is as friendly as ever, but he is sober, and he has come with a purpose: to get them to see the light, to free themselves from their illusions.

He has found happiness himself and wants the others to share it. But this happiness stems from the loss of his last illusion: he has realized that tomorrow holds no promise for him, and this is why he is at peace.

With his slick sales talk Hickey shakes his friends out of their twilight existence, provokes them, shocks them with his accusations that they are too cowardly to face the truth, and bewilders them with his promise of peace and contentment. Harry Hope and his pals resolve to look life in the face. One after another they go off to seek jobs. Hickey knows that they will not succeed, and he is right: the peace he has promised them is not forthcoming. Yet they still fail to realize that their only future is death. Their illusions return; they recover their taste for whiskey. Only the young anarchist who cannot forgive himself for betraying his mother takes the ultimate step and throws himself out of the window. Finally it comes out that Hickey has murdered his wife to put an end to the suffering he has caused her. His "call" to liberate the others from their illusions about life is seen to be a cloak to protect his own greater and more tragic illusion. The arrival of Hickey, the "iceman" or death, means the end of illusion, and hence the end of life.

Much in *The Iceman Cometh* derives from O'Neill's own experiences at Jimmy the Priest's dive on the New York waterfront, where a friend of his once committed suicide. Its similarity to Gorki's *The Lower Depths* is probably not coincidental, for O'Neill once said of this play that it "is really more wonderful propaganda for the submerged than any other play ever written, simply because it contains no propaganda, but rather shows humanity as it is—truth, in terms of human life." Yet the two plays present this truth in different ways.

Despite their similarities—in setting, character types, themes (escape from reality, the necessity of illusion), emphasis on dialogue rather than on action, situation (symbolic of the human condition), treatment of the central figure as catalyst—there remain important differences between the two plays: Gorki's play is socially oriented, designed to motivate social action, whereas O'Neill's play is psychologically oriented, designed to reveal the weakness or evil in man. *The Lower Depths* revolves around ethical problems of man in society, while *The Iceman Cometh* deals with the innate nature of the individual, the existential problems of the individual's flight from reality into the realm of illusion.

O'Neill's characters are not social outsiders proudly and deliberately avenging themselves on a social system they hate, but rather victims of their inherently human vulnerability to life-lies. This four-act play again combines symbolic and realistic elements. The language is realistic, sometimes brutal. The characterization is superb. Unlike most of O'Neill's other plays, *The Iceman Cometh* is not very experimental, unless the Ibsen-like tendency of concealing the motives of a central character until the end of the play can be called an experiment. In O'Neill's case, this delayed exposition requires that the audience, in spite of the extraordinary length of the play, reinterpret Hickey's words and actions in the light of the final disclosure.

In *The Iceman Cometh*, O'Neill rejected the

pseudo-Greek classicism of *Mourning Becomes Electra.*
At the heart of his play, there is neither the conflict
between divine will and human happiness, nor the
tragic flaw of the dramatic hero, but rather the paradox of the human condition in which dream is reality
and reality dream, in which despair becomes hope and
hope despair. Man is too frail to withstand the stark
truth of reality and must, in order to survive, renounce
it in favor of self-delusion. As Larry Slade, one of Harry
Hope's roomers, says:

"To hell with the truth! As the history of the world proves, the
truth has no bearing on anything. It's irrelevant and immaterial,
as the lawyers say. The lie of a pipe dream is what gives life to
the whole misbegotten mad lot of us, drunk or sober."

The element of tragedy, if it can be so called, arises
here not from a tragic flaw in the classical Greek sense,
but from the denial of one's illusions or pipe dreams.
Indebted, perhaps, to Schopenhauer or Freud, O'Neill
depicts the fundamental paradox of self-fulfillment
through annihilation. Hickey's guilt is not motivated by
revenge against an unfaithful wife. On the contrary,
his wife has been too faithful and too devoted. "That's
what made it so hard," admits Hickey, "That's what
made me feel such a rotten skunk—her always forgiv-
ing me." Hickey's criminal act is the result not of hatred
or vengence, but of his own inability to return the love
his wife had given him for so long. It is the recognition of this weakness or inadequacy, his self-admission
of the truth about himself, that brings about his crime.

Hickey seeks peace of mind in the destruction of

his last illusion, the illusion of his wife's infidelity with the iceman. But the end of illusion signals the end of life: "Do you suppose I give a damn about life now?" Hickey exclaims to the detective, "Why, you bonehead, I haven't got a single damned lying hope or pipe dream left!" In reality, there has been no iceman for his wife. Hickey himself has become the "iceman"—death, the destroyer of life-sustaining illusion.

Although *The Iceman Cometh* is perhaps too deliberately eschatological, too determined to avoid the superficial, O'Neill at least attempts to confront fundamental problems of human existence, to present in dramatic terms a tragic vision of life. In an article in *Life* of 2 December 1946, it was suggested that two conclusions can be drawn from this play: that great tragedy contradicts the spirit of American democracy, and that it is incompatible with the American belief in progress. This raises the question whether tragic greatness is possible in America, whether consciousness of evil, fear, and insecurity can be meaningfully treated, and whether such a meaningful artistic treatment can help man attain new dignity. *The Iceman Cometh* gives a negative answer, but *Long Day's Journey into Night* will show that this dignity is not unattainable—even in America.

Feeling unable to face the strain of a production, O'Neill said nothing about *The Iceman Cometh* for a time, but Lawrence Langner read it and thought it one of his best plays. When it opened in 1946 it brought only qualified praise. (Ten years later, however, when it was produced by José Quintero in New York in a re-

vival of O'Neill's works, it was recognized as an en-
richment of the American theater.) Leaving the cycle
aside, O'Neill now began work on *Long Day's Journey
into Night.*

8

The Compulsive Quest for Lost Time

Long Day's Journey into Night marks O'Neill's last phase. Putting technical experiment and "beautiful philosophy" behind him, he now looks back to the past, both his own and his family's, and tries to master it. *Long Day's Journey into Night* and *A Moon for the Misbegotten* are openly autobiographical; *A Touch of the Poet* contains a portrait of his father. Only in *More Stately Mansions* is the theme of family conflict treated more impersonally.

In his dedication of *Long Day's Journey into Night* to Carlotta, O'Neill called it a "play of old sorrow, written in tears and blood." The pathetic tone is suggestive of sentimentality with no claim to tragic depth, but anyone who reads or sees the play, with all its human suffering, anyone who knows that the "four haunted Tyrones" represent the four O'Neills, must be persuaded that it took more than artistic creativity to write this play and "finally look death in the face." O'Neill makes almost no attempt to disguise its autobiographical content—giving the family the name Tyrone is merely a formal gesture of dissociation. Many people who had known the O'Neills took this openness for a lack of natural filial respect, and this made the play all the more offensive to them. Those who believe that such considerations are relevant to artistic criticism should bear in mind that Edmund Tyrone (Eugene O'Neill) is depicted just as mercilessly as the other members of the family, and that from first to last the play shows compassion and understanding for all four of the haunted Tyrones.

O'Neill was reproached with having distorted facts,

with exaggerating old James Tyrone's stinginess, for example. From the human point of view this may be a
serious charge, but there can be no doubt that such
"distortions" intensified the drama. All memory is selec-
tive, especially when the events it recalls are occurring
in the mind of an experienced dramatist and seeking
appropriate expression.

   Long Day's Journey into Night presents four people, tortured by their inadequacies, whose only escape
is to mull over and magnify the faults of the others.
From time to time they make contact again in a moment of good will, only to fall back into mutual cruelty.
The father vacillates between love for his family and a
paralyzing fear of the poorhouse stemming from youth-
ful experiences. Mary, the convent-educated mother,
broken in spirit by her life on the road, her husband's
drinking and her own illness, is a morphine addict (al-
legedly because her husband never sent her to a good
doctor). James, the oldest son, is jealous of his younger
brother Edmund and devotes himself to drink and
women.

   The plot consists of the family's slow, reluctant
realization that Mary has relapsed after a promising
stay in an institution, and that Edmund, ill with tuberculosis, needs to be sent to a sanatorium. While they
try to maintain the family atmosphere of a home, they
split up their house into compartments, surround themselves with semitransparent screens—illusions through
which they observe each other. Mary cannot and will
not believe that Edmund is ill because this would mean
the fulfillment of a curse. James does not want to be-

lieve it because to do so would involve him in expense and bring him nearer to the poorhouse.

But in this play even illusions no longer offer an escape; they collapse or are destroyed. Truth breaks through in the form of words, but words die away and can be distorted. The Tyrones know that Mary sneaks off and takes morphine, but good manners demand that they ignore it. *Long Day's Journey into Night* culminates in a scene in which the three men, all drunk, watch Mary come downstairs dressed in her wedding dress, now entirely withdrawn into her own dream world of the past—the spirit of the Tyrones' illusions.

Long Day's Journey into Night combines most of O'Neill's major themes, but it surpasses most of the earlier treatments in one respect. Behind the wretchedness, avarice, nagging, and lies, one senses the dignity of the struggle to conquer despair. This dignity, which is unaffected by the success or failure of this struggle, makes the tragedy of the play believable.

Once again, O'Neill set the big cycle aside in order to work on something new: a series of one-acters entitled *By Way of Obit*. He quickly finished several drafts but never completed the series, of which only one play, *Hughie*, was published (in 1959). This is a minimally dramatized short story, without plot but even richer in atmosphere than the early sea plays. In contrast to such a play as *The Moon of the Caribbees*, however, *Hughie* is colorless, makes little use of sound effects, and lacks the profusion of characters.

It presents two men, the night clerk of a third-class hotel and one of its seedy residents, who meet in the lobby. Having little in common except their mediocrity, they are brought together by boredom and chance. A conversation develops, or rather a monologue by the guest, encouraged by an occasional "Yes" or "Is that so?" from the other man. Only at the end does the night clerk awaken to some extent into the present, when the professional mask behind which he sleeps is slightly disarranged. But this does not mean that the action gets any livelier. The night clerk is asleep; the whole building is asleep; the guest is on his way to bed. The monologue drags on—and yet what happens on stage is far from static. If the play were longer this might not be true, but as it is there is a feeling of great intensity, the atmosphere of the Hell Hole (one of O'Neill's favorite saloons) at nighttime, a sense of impending death, of peeling wallpaper and a crumbling hotel.

Hughie is no more than an unfinished sketch, and this increases its appeal, for this is what keeps it alive, though its action seems to be taking place in a state of apparent semiconsciousness. We know almost nothing of O'Neill's intentions concerning this play's place in the projected series, but it gives us good reason to regret that more of these "fingerprints of a moment" were not written down.

During World War II, O'Neill's forgiveness of the four haunted Tyrones was obviously not enough to master the agonizing memories that plagued him. In his next play, *A Moon for the Misbegotten*, a statement as open and outspoken as *Long Day's Journey into Night*, he made a final attempt to reconcile himself to his past.

James Tyrone (Jamie O'Neill) is courting Josie, an oversize woman who has come to think of herself as the village slut. Behind her unconscious attempt to compensate for her physical ungainliness through her "brazen trollop act," James recognizes her purity and warm maternal heart. His own mother has recently died, and in Josie he finds the mother figure he is seeking. When he is with her, his tenseness relaxes. He tells her the story of his transcontinental trip bringing his mother's body east for burial. The encounter of these two self-deceptive figures ends in mutual confession and self-understanding.

A Moon for the Misbegotten seems more personal than *Long Day's Journey into Night*; it arises from O'Neill's desire to come to terms with the events it describes. But it would be wrong to censure it on the ground that the stage was no place to air his family's problems. Thematically, the play is as valid as any other O'Neill ever wrote, and its two main characters are presented as human beings in a dilemma both timeless and universal. Yet *A Moon for the Misbegotten* is extraordinarily difficult to stage. It suffers from a certain awkward juxtaposition of serious and comic elements and from an inability to portray the minor roles convincingly. Written, as it were, in the shadow of *Long Day's Journey into Night*, it is eclipsed by that play.

In February 1944 the O'Neills gave up Tao House and moved into a hotel in San Francisco. Although O'Neill had four plays ready for production, he insisted on waiting until the war was over. At the end of 1945 rehearsals for *The Iceman Cometh* began, and the

O'Neills went to New York. There, after years of relative seclusion, contact with old friends and work with the Theater Guild brought O'Neill to life again. But a production of *Long Day's Journey into Night* remained out of the question. He deposited the play under seal with his publisher Bennett Cerf with instructions that it was not to be published until twenty-five years after his death.

On 9 October 1946, *The Iceman Cometh* opened at the Martin Beck Theater in New York. Despite the generally positive reviews and George Jean Nathan's warm praise, there were complaints about the play's excessive length and repetitiousness. O'Neill's popularity, which had suffered from the long period of time during which no new plays by him had appeared on the New York stage, was not markedly enhanced. And *A Moon for the Misbegotten* did not reach Broadway (until 1957), although it was performed several times off Broadway. Censors began complaining of its immorality, and in Detroit it was closed by the police.

As a result of illness, O'Neill was gradually forced to cease writing. His deteriorating physical condition left him hardly able to light a cigarette or sign a letter. After a short convalescence in the hospital, he and Carlotta moved first into a small, seaside house near Boston, then into a Boston hotel. O'Neill had become a helpless invalid, and his physical weakness precluded creative work. During this time, he decided to destroy all drafts and manuscripts of his extensive cycle, except *A Touch of the Poet* and a bulky draft of *More Stately Mansions*.

Early in November 1953 O'Neill developed pneumonia. He had no physical resistence left, and after a long and painful struggle he died in his Boston hotel on 27 November 1953. Yet this was not the end of his career. The public and the critics could still look forward to two plays of his projected cycle, *A Touch of the Poet* and the unfinished *More Stately Mansions*, as well as *Hughie* and the sealed manuscript of *Long Day's Journey into Night*. Through the help of the Secretary General of the United Nations, Dag Hammarskjöld, Karl Ragnar Gierow, director of the Stockholm Royal Dramatic Theater, who had done much to popularize O'Neill in Sweden and other European countries, secured the production rights to *Long Day's Journey into Night*. It appears doubtful whether O'Neill would have agreed to the premature production, but Carlotta claimed that shortly before his death he had presented it to the Royal Dramatic Theater.

Be that as it may, the Stockholm production of 1956 stimulated a strong revival of interest in O'Neill. *Long Day's Journey into Night* was immediately recognized as a masterpiece, and there were several more productions, including one with an excellent cast in New York that same year. Many critics considered it O'Neill's best work, a judgment that was confirmed by the posthumous award of his fourth Pulitzer Prize.

Encouraged by this success, Gierow produced *A Touch of the Poet* in Stockholm the following year (1957). As O'Neill originally planned his cycle, this play—one of the most taut and structurally unified work from his later period—deals with the intrusion of

Sara Melody, daughter of a disgraced Irish army officer, into the aristocratic New England Harford family. Cornelius Melody is set apart from other people by "a touch of the poet"—a sense of style which he maintains at all cost. He keeps a horse which he cannot afford; his old officer's uniform bolsters his self-importance. This ex-officer, forced to resign his commission and to emigrate to the United States, where he makes a meager living as proprietor of a cheap saloon, stands before a mirror reciting Byron. In the mirror he sees an officer in military bearing, a Byronic figure. He plays his role against the shabby background of the world he lives in, fighting for his illusions. At his side is his wife Nora, a passively suffering, loving wife, ready to believe and forgive anything. She loves him both for what he is and for what he would like to be. At his other side is his cool-headed daughter Sara, who seems to despise his bluff and his weakness, and tries to strip away his mask.

Skillfully implanted within this triangle is the germ from which the action of the rest of the cycle will spring. Simon Harford, rejected by his family and full of ideas for reforming the world, is living in a cottage near the Melodys' house. He falls in love with Sara, who is taking care of him during an illness. (In *A Touch of the Poet* Simon Harford is only an offstage character, although he becomes a key figure in the later development of the cycle.) The Harford family contemptuously reject the idea of a marriage between Sara and Simon, and try to bribe Sara to leave the neighborhood. Major Melody's pretensions become uncontrollable; he feels that his honor as an officer is at

stake and in a ludicrous gesture of desperation chal-
lenges Harford to a duel. He is beaten up by Harford's
manservant and banished from the premises. With his
pride destroyed, Melody drops his mask and recognizes
himself for what he is. In a scene of tremendous tension, he rushes out to the stable to shoot not himself
but his mare, the symbol of his pride and social position. Through his struggle, which is as authentic as that
of the Tyrones, he becomes a truly tragic character and
thus arouses our pity. The figure of Major Melody, who
embodies many features of James O'Neill, is one of the
few characters in the American playwright's work who
manages to escape from his self-woven network of pretensions and to accept life realistically and honestly.
And in so doing, he attains a freedom from illusion similar to that advocated in Hickey's "philosophy" in *The
Iceman Cometh*.

The climax when Major Melody stands before us,
transformed, humiliated but honest, actually marks the
end of the plot, but O'Neill follows it with a second
more subtle climax whose significance was to become
crucial in the later plays of the cycle: the acknowledg-
ment of his true self proves to be what Sara had always wanted of her father. This demonstration of cour-
age and honesty instantly changes her attitude. In her
proud insistence on truth and honesty, Major Melody's
old pride flares up in his daughter.

Without knowing it, Sara, like her father, also has
"a touch of the poet." For her it is unbearable not to be
the daughter of a major. The complications inherent in
this situation are developed in the later plays of the

cycle, as Sara seeks her own salvation. The area in
which this will take place is indicated in one of the
most poignant scenes of the play: the clash between
Sara and Simon's mother, Deborah. These two women
and Simon form the triangle from which the dramatic
conflict of *More Stately Mansions* stems.

In 1958, Gierow produced the one-act *Hughie* in
Stockholm, which by this time had become an O'Neill
center. The supply of performable posthumous plays
now seemed to be exhausted, but Gierow, who believed
that O'Neill had deliberately refrained from destroy-
ing the fragmentary manuscript of *More Stately Mansions*, undertook to cut this version of the play, which
would have run for about nine hours, to a manageable
length. (Additional notes to *More Stately Mansions*
found later were used by Gierow in producing the
Stockholm version of the play.) He was forced to eliminate some of the characters in the complex plot and
had to make additional cuts to fit the play together
again. The action now centers on three characters:
Simon Harford, his wife Sara, and his mother Deborah.

The critics, who had come to Stockholm from all
over the world for this last O'Neill premiere, naturally
had to be cautious and reserved in evaluating the play
as it stood. There were two obstacles to a reliable evaluation: *More Stately Mansions* was not a finished play
but an evolutionary phase, and the manuscript was
not available for comparison with the condensed version performed in Stockholm. Yet even this abbreviated
version was considered too long. The Swedish critic
Göran O. Eriksson said that although it gripped the

audience for almost its entire length "you are glad and relieved when it is over, because by that time it has almost driven you mad" (*Göteborgs Handels och Sjö-farts Tidning*, 10 November 1962).

Gierow's version takes up the story four years after the events presented in *A Touch of the Poet*. Simon Harford has given up his Rousseauesque plans for reforming the world in order to manage the almost bankrupt family business, and instead becomes a brutal, successful industrialist. Once again the tragedy of an O'Neill character stems from the conflict between truth and self-deception. Simon himself sees his excursion into exploitation as a step toward realizing his dream: a world of true equality where exploitation does not exist. But if he ever was an idealist, he is one no longer. Life has become a constant resolving of conflicts between what he does not have and what he wants—and the way he solves the conflict is by taking. He falls into the life philosophy of *The Great God Brown*: to be strong is to be good, and to be strong means to possess. Just as Brown's philosophy came to grief over Margaret, Simon is destroyed by the two women who are supposed to be his very source of life. He wants to possess both of them simultaneously, Deborah as a mother and Sara as wife and mistress, but they resist being possessed. They elude him or merge into a single person or crush him in their irreconcilable struggle to gain sole domination over him. What makes the play unbearable is the hopelessness and inexorability of this perpetual triangular conflict, which grows more and more complex, brutal and dominating. There are intervals of peace when everybody's possessive demands seem to have been satisfied in an illusory compromise, but these are no more than exhausted breathing spells before a new phase of the battle begins. Sara knowingly drives Deborah into schizophrenia; Simon's despondent mother escapes into the happiness of her courtesan's dream world. Her schizophrenia is ultimately Simon's, too. He cherishes the illusion that he can live a harmonious life as a good son to his mother and at the same time a good lover to Sara, ideally reconciling all possessiveness. Sara goes along with the pretense that her love can be bought—a mask which she soon finds herself unable to cast off, for the game both disgusts and fascinates her.

In all three characters of *More Stately Mansions*, love (whether maternal or sexual) is transformed into desire to possess. The self is surrendered to this desire, and the result is a struggle for mutual enslavement fought with whatever weapons are available, to the point of contemplated murder—a struggle for possession which never brings victory but only inner impoverishment and ultimately loss of identity. As is often the case in O'Neill, the play ends with a formal solution, which is easily misunderstood. Deborah gives up the struggle and retreats for good into her dream world. Sara, now both mistress and mother, is left as the sole possessor of Simon. In a trancelike state in which he reverts to his childhood, he accepts her as his mother. But this is not the end of the story. The trance will pass. The play has simply reached the point of utter exhaustion. O'Neill did not live to write the word "Curtain."

9

Conclusion

Even in the second half of the twentieth century, performances of O'Neill's work have continued to raise new questions concerning America's greatest dramatist, new world drama, and even modern drama as a whole. After his early successes he was recognized as a great talent, and it was assumed that he would go on to become a master. But his development as a dramatist was not dictated by any logic deducible from the development of modern drama. It was not merely a matter of a more mature craftsmanship or a greater consolidation of a philosophical *Weltanschauung*. Recent decades have seen many attempts to force the phenomenon of O'Neill into the framework of an unambiguous system of ideas like the ones to which Ibsen, Pirandello, and Brecht lend themselves. But any such attempt must confine itself to one single phase or aspect of his work. At various points in his career the "definitive" O'Neill seemed to have emerged, yet invariably within a short time the restless, insatiable experimenter was at work again. It is not simply a case of failing to reach a final judgment since, after all, in art there never can be a final judgment. With O'Neill, we have not even been able to bring into focus his fundamental idea or the essentials of his artistic position.

When we look at this dramatist's voluminous work within the context of contemporary ideologies, literary currents, and fashions, we recognize so much that is already familiar, so much that has already been more forcefully expressed and more meaningfully demonstrated that we have no recourse but to revise our impression of O'Neill as an elusive loner. Is his work then just a conglomerate of ideas adopted from other writers and held together by his instinctive theatrical sense? Could it be that his great achievement was not so much to have written timeless, enduring works as to have played a great historical role in breaking new ground for a decaying theatrical tradition of superficiality and commercialism? Did he break out the windows of an established American theater in order to let in the light of European drama? Many critics believe so. In 1932, the English critic and dramatist St. John Ervine said that O'Neill was merely America's Marlowe, preparing the way for its Shakespeare. Such facetious judgments, applicable only to some nonexistent figure, reveal the uncertainty of some critics, even those of the stature of St. John Ervine, in attempting to come to grips with the O'Neill phenomenon.

In relating O'Neill to his forerunners and contemporaries as well as to literary trends abroad, some characteristics of O'Neill's work offer points of departure. Up to *Beyond the Horizon*, his early plays show the same painstaking, detailed realism of European naturalistic drama and the determinism and positivism of Zola. Even here the "pipe dream" theme, so close to Ibsen's "life-sustaining lie," which will recur again and again until the closing movements of *More Stately Mansions*, is already emerging. The programmatic suggestions O'Neill made to the Provincetown group show that even as a young man he believed the most effective contemporary dramatic styles to be those of Ibsen and Strindberg. The references in his Nobel Prize speech to Strindberg as the master of modern dramatists, the monologue technique in *Before Breakfast*, the love-hate relationship of the husband and wife in *Welded*, the mutual castigation of the Tyrones in *Long Day's Journey into Night*—all this provided considerable justification for regarding O'Neill as a belated American Strindberg. But in the course of O'Neill's development, Strindbergian elements were no more lasting than naturalism, and they do not dominate his mature work.

Attempts to define his artistic personality rely to a surprising degree on simplistic generalizations which relegate him to a subsidiary, derivative position and reduce his dramaturgy to a convenient formula. He has been called, for example, the American Georg Kaiser. Unquestionably he did go through an Expressionistic phase, in which certain techniques and themes approximated those of the German Expressionists. Yet despite the numerous similarities between O'Neill and Kaiser, there remains an important distinction between these two playwrights: O'Neill was primarily concerned not with the rebirth of man through social revolution, but rather with the fate of individuals, whose existence and problems are not confined to any particular social structure. His heated reaction to criticism of *The Hairy Ape* as a play of social propaganda stressed a point that holds true for his work in general: he was not an exponent of George Bernard Shaw's sober brand of social propaganda or of the rhetorical social protest of many Expressionists. His work, written at a time when social criticism dominated the arts, shows an almost anachronistic indifference to such matters of intellectual fashion.

Yet to regard this as a virtue in itself would be to negate the element of socio-historical relevance which prevents art from floating in a timeless void. We have to admit that O'Neill as a thinker is often weak, unreliable and superficial. He has been called "a peddler of second-hand ideas," and even if this criticism overstresses the ideological content of his plays, there can be no doubt that he frequently faltered whenever he tried to be profoundly philosophical or "modern," whenever he entered the realm of abstract ideas. Along with James Joyce, Thomas Mann, and Hermann Broch, he participated in the rediscovery of myth initiated by T. S. Eliot, but his attempt to "psychologize" the Greek tragedians' concept of fate resulted in the Zolaesque determinism of *Mourning Becomes Electra.* Not only does his study of women in *Strange Interlude* exceed the limits of an individual psyche, but the play itself, with its somewhat awkward dramatization of the stream-of-consciousness technique, exceeds the limits of effective theater. Yet to dismiss O'Neill for his lack of skill in developing ideas presupposes that his plays are to be judged primarily as vehicles for ideas. Like Joyce, O'Neill has often been evaluated on this basis, but his best works are no more plays of ideas than are García Lorca's tragedies.

Few elements in O'Neill's dramatic style remain constant throughout his work. Early in his career he revealed his extraordinary gift for lending a dramatic, articulate force to slang, the speech of the inarticulate. His farmers, seamen, bums, and prostitutes, like the Irish peasants in J. M. Synge, speak a language of po-

etic musicality, full of unexpected naive, oblique
images, which often fail to crystallize. One critic
charged, with some justification, that O'Neill often confused the forcefulness of this language with the forcefulness of its expletives. In many of his plays he develops a consistency of tone, a musical unity. The tone
of hauntedness that pervades *Long Day's Journey into
Night* characterizes also *The Emperor Jones,* where it
takes on an explicitly musical form, produced by the
use of sound, especially drums. Most of the plays con-
tain rhythmic repetitions of what might be called a
refrain; in *Lazarus Laughed* the "musical" laughter of
the liberated Lazarus serves this function. Besides this
musical tendency to dispense with words, O'Neill also
displays an affinity for film techniques. The use of
masks in *The Great God Brown,* for example, obviously
owes much to careful study of the possibilities of the
motion-picture camera. The cinematographic medium
is far more suitable than the conventional stage for con-
veying the dramatic effect of all the differentiated
crowd scenes in *Lazarus Laughed.* The same applies
to the minute detail of O'Neill's stage directions, which
only the camera could properly translate into visual
terms.

One characteristic is consistently evident throughout O'Neill's career: an unusual technical flexibility,
a readiness to experiment and take risks, which he
never lost even in his later years. His plays explore the
full range of dramatic expression, which continued to
fascinate him as long as he lived. Parallel to this runs
his experimentation with ideas. Many writers have left

their mark, stylistic or philosophical, on his work; they include Spengler, Nietzsche, Marx, Freud, Aeschylus, Shakespeare, Ibsen, Strindberg, Gerhart Hauptmann, and Georg Kaiser. While O'Neill's work in its totality indicates chaos and helplessness, the individual plays show a tentative reaching out, quickly overcome, toward nihilism and Catholicism, determinism and the triumph of human freedom. This is what St. John Ervine meant when he said that O'Neill does not develop, he just expands. But it was precisely this infinite reluctance to declare or commit himself that constituted the artistic as well as the philosophical and religious freedom so indispensable to O'Neill. This predilection for epic completeness—or rather "all-embracingness"—is just as evident in the total *œuvre* as in the individual later plays and dramatic cycles, which can no longer be contained within conventional limits. It is a characteristic O'Neill shares with James Joyce, Hermann Broch, and Robert Musil. He was no more capable than the author of *Finnegans Wake* of complying with Ervine's demand that he adopt a final artistic position, formally and philosophically.

To look for O'Neill's enduring value in his flexibility and his adroit acrobatic (often superficial) handling of ideas—the sort of relative value that Joyce enjoys—may seem questionable. Nevertheless his great works are best approached, not by way of his technical experiments or his "ideas," but by insight into an experience of life almost untouched by ideas and mastered only through the imposition of artistic form. The quality of a play like *Long Day's Journey into Night*

stemmed from personal suffering rather than from a
dramatic idea. O'Neill's often unique experiments may
prove to be dated, but his best plays, with their spon-
taneity and confessional intensity, are genuine and
powerful expressions of the spiritual anguish, helplessness, lies, and mutual human destruction, which O'Neill
 knew only too well. They give us a glimpse of the man
behind the experimenter, suffering and sacrificing himself to art. This is what distinguishes O'Neill from any
fashions, trends, or movements to which he may have
subscribed or with which he may have been identified.

Chronology

1888:	Born October 16 in New York City.
1888–1895:	Road tours with his parents.
1896–1907:	Formal education at Mount St. Vincent-on-Hudson School (New York), De La Salle Military Institute (New York), Betts Academy (Conn.), and Princeton University.
1909:	Marriage to Kathleen Jenkins. Gold-prospecting expedition to Honduras.
1910–1911:	Voyages to Buenos Aires and Durban, South Africa. Return to U.S. aboard a British steamer.
1911–1912:	At Jimmy the Priest's in New York.
1912:	Divorce from Kathleen Jenkins, Cub reporter on the New London (Conn.) *Telegraph*.
1912–1913:	At Gaylord Farm sanatorium. Wrote first one-act plays.
1914:	First publication: *Thirst, and Other One-Act Plays*.
1914–1915:	At Professor G. P. Baker's "Workshop 47" (Harvard).
1916:	*Bound East for Cardiff* (Provincetown, Mass.), *Thirst* (Provincetown), *Before Breakfast*.

Includes the first productions of O'Neill's plays. Unless otherwise indicated, the place of production is New York City.

1917:   *Fog, The Sniper, In the Zone, The Long Voyage
           Home, Ile.*
1918:   Marriage to Agnes Boulton. *The Rope, Where the
           Cross Is Made, The Moon of the Caribbees.*
1919:   *The Dreamy Kid.*
1920:   *Beyond the Horizon, Chris Christopherson* (At-
           lantic City; early version of *Anna Christie*), *Exor-
           cism, The Emperor Jones, Diff'rent.* Awarded the
           Pulitzer Prize for *Beyond the Horizon.*
1921:   *Gold, Anna Christie, The Straw.*
1922:   *The First Man, The Hairy Ape.* Awarded the
           Pulitzer Prize for *Anna Christie.*
1924:   *Welded, The Ancient Mariner* (Provincetown), *All
           God's Chillun Got Wings* (Provincetown), *S. S.
           Glencairn* (Provincetown), *Desire under the Elms.*
1925:   *The Fountain.*
1926:   *The Great God Brown.*
1928:   *Marco Millions, Strange Interlude, Lazarus Laughed*
           (Pasadena, Cal.). Extended trip to Europe and Asia
           with Carlotta Monterey. Awarded the Pulitzer Prize
           for *Strange Interlude.*
1929:   *Dynamo.* Divorce from Agnes Boulton. Marriage
           to Carlotta Monterey.
1931:   *Mourning Becomes Electra.*
1933:   *Ah, Wilderness!.*
1934:   *Days without End.*
1936:   Nobel Prize for Literature.
1946:   *The Iceman Cometh.*
1947:   *A Moon for the Misbegotten* (Columbus, Ohio).
1953:   Died on November 27 in Boston.
1956:   *Long Day's Journey into Night* (Stockholm).
1957:   *A Touch of the Poet* (Stockholm). Awarded the
           Pulitzer Prize for *Long Day's Journey into Night.*
1958:   *Hughie* (Stockholm).
1962:   *More Stately Mansions* (Stockholm).

Works by Eugene O'Neill

Thirst, and Other One-Act Plays (1914);

Before Breakfast (1916);

The Moon of the Caribbees, and Six Other Plays of the Sea (1919);

Beyond the Horizon (1920);

Gold (1921);

The Emperor Jones, Diff'rent, The Straw (1921);

The Hairy Ape, Anna Christie, The First Man (1922);

All God's Chillun Got Wings, and Welded (1924);

The Complete Works of Eugene O'Neill (2 vols., 1924);

Desire under the Elms (1925);

Plays (4 vols., 1925);

The Great God Brown, The Fountain, The Moon of the Caribbees, and Other Plays (1926);

Lazarus Laughed (1927);

Marco Millions (1927);

Strange Interlude (1928);

Dynamo (1929);

Mourning Becomes Electra (1931);

Collected Poems (Part 3 of *A Bibliography of the Works of Eugene O'Neill*, ed. R. Sanborn and B. H. Clark, 1931);

Nine Plays (1932);

Ah, Wilderness! (1933);

Days without End (1934);

The Plays Eugene O'Neill (12 vols., 1934–1935);

The Iceman Cometh (1946);

Lost Plays of Eugene O'Neill (1950);

The Plays of Eugene O'Neill (3 vols., 1951);

A Moon for the Misbegotten (1952);

Long Day's Journey into Night (1956);

A Touch of the Poet (1957);

Hughie (1959);

More Stately Mansions (1964);

Ten "Lost" Plays (1964).

Bibliographical Notes

The earliest biography of O'Neill, Barrett Clark's *Eugene O'Neill: The Man and His Plays* (New York, 1926), was written with O'Neill's collaboration. Although its critical value is limited, it is useful because it contains letters and factual material authorized by O'Neill himself.

Two books dealing with O'Neill's life are helpful providing the facts are carefully checked: *Part of a Long Story* (New York, 1958) by O'Neill's second wife, Agnes Boulton, which treats of the period between 1917 and 1919, and Croswell Bowen's *The Curse of the Misbegotten* (New York, 1959). Arthur and Barbara Gelb's exhaustive biography *O'Neill* (New York, 1960), the most complete biographical study of O'Neill to date, often obscures the playwright's essential features, due to its excessive detail and somewhat indiscriminating comprehensiveness. Yet its scope and thoroughness recommend it as an important and indispensable contribution to O'Neill scholarship.

Louis Sheaffer's *O'Neill: Son and Playwright* (Boston, 1968), the first volume of a two-part biographical study (to be completed in 1971), traces the first half of O'Neill's life up to the 1920 production of *Beyond the Horizon*. It is a reliable, objective, and well-documented discussion of O'Neill's relationships with his family and an investigation of the autobiographical sources of his plays. It focuses on O'Neill's family, friends,

and acquaintances who were the models for his dramatic characters, rather than on the way in which O'Neill presented these
characters on stage.

As early as 1935 Richard Dana Skinner attempted a fundamental evaluation of O'Neill's work in *Eugene O'Neill: A Poet's
Quest* (New York, 1935). Skinner interprets it from a Roman
Catholic point of view as a quest for the true faith that reached
its objective in the confessional *Days without End*—an interpretation contradicted by the later plays. *The Haunted Heroes of
Eugene O'Neill* by Edwin A. Engel (Cambridge, Mass., 1953)
makes a useful contribution to the clarification of O'Neill's
philosophical views, as does Doris Falk's psychoanalytical *Eugene
O'Neill and the Tragic Tension* (New Brunswick, N.J., 1958).

Several other books deserve special attention: the second
edition of Sophus Keith Winther's *Eugene O'Neill: A Critical
Study* (New York, 1961), a sympathetic critique of O'Neill's
work; Doris Alexander's *The Tempering of Eugene O'Neill*
(New York, 1962), an excellent study of O'Neill's coming of age
as an artist; Clifford Leech's *O'Neill* (New York, 1963); Frederic
Carpenter's *Eugene O'Neill* in Twayne's "United States Authors"
series (New York, 1964); and John Gassner's *Eugene O'Neill*
in the University of Minnesota "Pamphlets on American Writers"
series (Minneapolis, 1965).

John Henry Raleigh's penetrating analysis of the O'Neill
Weltanschauung in *The Plays of Eugene O'Neill* (Carbondale,
Ill.) was published in 1965. In 1968, two specialized studies
appeared: Chester Clayton Long's *The Role of Nemesis in the
Structure of Selected Plays by Eugene O'Neill* (New York);
and Timo Tiusanen's *O'Neill's Scenic Images* (Princeton), an
interesting analysis of the interdependence of the verbal and
scenic means of expression in O'Neill's plays. Egil Törnqvist's
*A Drama of Souls: Studies in O'Neill's Super-Naturalistic Tech-
nique* (Uppsala, 1968), a discussion of O'Neill's treatment of
the supernatural in terms of his dramatic devices and stagecraft,
is another important study.

Two valuable collections of essays offer a representative
selection of O'Neill criticism. *O'Neill and His Plays*, edited by

Oscar Cargill, N. Bryllion Fagin, and William J. Fisher (New York, 1961), contains contributions by George Jean Nathan, Sean O'Casey, T. S. Eliot, George Pierce Baker, and Karl Ragnar Gierow, as well as an extensive bibliography. The second collection is *O'Neill: A Collection of Essays*, edited by John Gassner (Englewood Cliffs, N.J., 1964).

The author of the present book wishes to express his thanks to Hans-Joachim Schulz and Richard Schroeder for their valuable help.

Index